The Lives

of the

Christmas
Music Makers

by

Dale V. Nobbman

ISBN 978-1-57424-374-1

Copyright ©2018 CENTERSTREAM Publishing
P. O. Box 17878 - Anaheim Hills, CA 92817
email: centerstrm@aol.com • web: centerstream-usa.com
714-779-9390

THE LIVES of the CHRISTMAS MUSIC MAKERS

A look into the lives of the authors, composers, and translators of our favorite pre-20th century traditional *'Christmas Songs Heard Around the World'*

This book provides comprehensive biographical sketches of the men and women who wrote, composed, and translated the most famous *traditional* Christmas songs of all-time. Many of these individuals rose above poverty, physical handicaps and other adversities to eventually write their names in the music history books. We know their music very well, but this book gives music history buffs fresh insight into the lives of these men and women. Their true-life stories and achievements are fascinating and inspirational for anyone wanting to know more about the people behind the music.

Their songs have left a legacy of joy, happiness, and pleasant memories for generations of people around the world, and as a result, Christmas carols and hymns have very possibly become the most influential body of music in the Western world. At the very least, these songs return year-after-year for an encore performance each November and December, and we anxiously look forward to hearing them once again.

Christmastime can be a depressing time for some people, but who hasn't been uplifted by Christmas music at some point in their lives? I know these songs have been inspirational for me, from my earliest years, and I have a feeling you will view the songs you sing this Christmas with renewed appreciation after reading about the men and women who created them. There has never been a book featuring so much factual information about the lives of these poets and musicians; complete with their pictures or portraits.

Just as men who were "carried along by the Holy Spirit," wrote the Bible, I believe the men and women featured in this book received *special inspiration* to create our beloved traditional Christmas songs which have survived the test of time. Just think about it for a moment; it took literally *hundreds* of years to complete some of our favorite songs as we know them today. I feel that took a lot of musical 'orchestration' from above.

Finally, after all these years, the men and women connected with our Christmas music can now take 'a collective bow' for their positive contributions to our world, and we in return can applaud them with a well-deserved thank you of appreciation for their work.

Dale V. Nobbman

This book is dedicated to Jesus Christ.
He is the reason Christians
celebrate the Christmas season.

The Christmas Story in Song

It came upon the midnight clear,
while shepherds watched their flocks by night
that angels we have heard on high
proclaimed joy to the world!
For away in a manger there is
born to you this day, in the city of David,
a Savior who is Christ the Lord.
And as the angels from the realms
of glory witnessed the first noel,
hark the herald angels did sing
oh come, oh come Emmanuel and
oh come all ye faithful to see what child is this?
Go tell it on the mountain that
it is the sweet little Jesus boy,
born on this silent night, oh holy night,
in the little town of Bethlehem.

by

Dale V. Nobbman

This 'Christmas Story in Song' was written primarily
using 16 traditional Christmas song titles.
Can you name the songs?

BIOGRAPHIES

ADOLPHE CHARLES ADAM

Composer of music for "O Holy Night" in 1847

Born on July 24, 1803 in Paris, France
Died on May 3, 1856 in Paris, France

Adolphe Adam was the son of a music professor and professional pianist, Jean Louis Adam, and Elisabethe (Coste). His father tried his best to dissuade his son from pursuing a musical career and become a lawyer. Eventually, his father gave in to his son's musical interest and allowed Adolphe to study music. Adolphe would later describe his father as the 'founder of the French school of piano playing.'

As a child, Adolphe preferred to improvise music of his own rather than study music seriously. His formal training began in boarding school, before entering the Paris Conservatoire in 1819, where his father taught music from 1797-1842. By age twenty Adolphe was writing songs for vaudeville houses in Paris and was playing in the Gymnase Orchestra, where he would later become the chorus master. He had his first one-act opera produced at the 'Opera-Comique' in 1829. By 1830, Adolphe had completed 28 theater works and had made himself such a name in the music world that he was invited to London in 1832 to provide the music for a spectacle at Covent Garden, where his brother-in-law was the musical director. In 1839 he was in St. Petersburg, Russia, to provide music for the court of Tsar Nicholas I. Adolphe returned to Paris and produced his most famous music for the ballet 'Giselle,' which premiered at the Paris Opera on June 28, 1841.

Adolphe wrote the music for "O Holy Night" in early December of 1847, just prior to a financially bad year for himself in 1848. Adolphe had co-established a new opera house in Paris, the Opera-National, in 1847, for which he had secured a considerable loan for the project. The timing for the venture proved not to be the best, for in 1848 political disturbances in France, and throughout Europe, forced the closure of his theater, and it took him until 1853 to pay off his debts. Fortunately, for us Christmas music lovers, Adolphe composed the music for "O Holy Night" at the peak of his musical composition career, just before his financial ruin, which forced him to turn to journalism and the academic world to earn a living. It would have to be viewed as more than luck that a man of the Jewish faith would compose the music to a Christmas hymn for a holiday that he didn't celebrate and which contained words that he did not necessarily believe. God does work in mysterious ways and nowhere is this more evident than in the study of the creation of many of our favorite Christmas hymns.

In 1849, the year of his father's death, Adolphe was appointed a professor of composition at the Paris Conservatoire, where he served until his sudden death from an apparent heart attack in 1856. He had written 39 operas, 14 ballets, and 80 stage works. Several of his comic operas were presented in America, with the first being performed in New York City in 1839.

In his posthumously published autobiographical sketches, Adolphe admitted that it was his work as a musician that was his sole passion and pleasure, without which he would have died from boredom. Thankfully, Adolphe's sole passion in life gave us the beautiful "O Holy Night."

CECIL FRANCES HUMPHREYS ALEXANDER

Author of "Once In Royal David's City" in 1848

Born in April 1818 in County Tyrone, Ireland
Died on October 12, 1895 in Londonderry, England

Cecil (Humphreys) Alexander was the third child of Major John Humphreys of the Royal Marines and his wife Elizabeth (Reed). Cecil was born nearsighted and shy by nature, and began writing poetry at the age of nine. Because her father was a soldier and a rather stern man, young Cecil was not sure that he would be pleased with her poetry, and therefore hid her poems under a carpet. One day in 1832 her father noticed a bulge under the floor covering and discovered a batch of papers on which his daughter had written verses. It turned out that he was touched by her poems and took them to the renowned clergyman-poet, John Keble, who read them and proclaimed Cecil a 'born writer.' Cecil's father encouraged her writing more poetry by having the family gather for an hour every Saturday evening, at which time he would read her latest poems.

In October of 1850, Cecil married William Alexander, who at the time was serving a parish spread out over miles of mountains in Ireland. William was six years younger than Cecil and this was cause of concern to her family, and that is why sometimes her birth-date is published as 1823 or 1825, instead of the actual 1818. Cecil proved to be a faithful churchwoman, who day after day rode over the moorlands in all kinds of weather to carry food, warm clothing and medical supplies to the impoverished and sick. William became a bishop in 1867 and meanwhile Cecil found the time to write 400 hymns and poems, most of them for children.

Cecil's most famous works appeared in her song collections 'Verses for Holy Seasons' in 1846, and 'Hymns for Little Children' in 1848, with an introduction by her early writing admirer, John Keble. Other than "Once In Royal David's City," her best-known hymn is "There Is A Green Hill Far Away" written in 1848 and sung at both her funeral in 1895 and that of William's in 1911. Her 1856 poem "Burial of Moses" was one of the few poems by a living author that the famous poet, Tennyson, professed he wished he had written.

"Once In Royal David's City" was published in 1848 with the purpose of interpreting for children the clause in the Apostles' Creed, "(I believe) in Jesus Christ, our Lord, who was born of the Virgin Mary." Henry Gauntlett composed the music in 1849 for this poem written by Cecil for her godchildren Unfortunately, Cecil never managed to meet Mr. Gauntlett in person. She died one month after suffering a stroke in 1895.

Writing songs intended for the Christmas season was primarily 'a man's job' until nearly the second half of the 20th century. Prior to the time Cecil wrote the words for this hymn it is virtually impossible to find a Christmas song authored by a woman! This makes Cecil a true 'pioneer' in the writing of popular Christmas music, alongside Christina Rossetti. Included in this group would be the great female translator of German hymns, Catherine Winkworth, and poet Emily Huntington Miller, these four ladies are the only women I know of to produce gender breaking literary work through Christmas songs of lasting popularity from the 19th century.

PHILLIPS BROOKS

Author of "O Little Town of Bethlehem" in 1868

Born on December 13, 1835 in Boston, Massachusetts
Died on January 23, 1893 in Boston, Massachusetts

Phillips Brooks was the second of six sons born to a Boston merchant couple, William Gray and Mary Ann (Phillips) Brooks, and his ancestry on both sides goes back to the 17th century Puritans in America. His father's lineage is traced back to the Rev. John Cotton, who is known as the 'Patriarch of New England.' William Gray Brooks and family joined the Protestant Episcopal Church when Phillips was twelve, in response to growing Unitarianism in Congregational churches. Phillips's family was not very musical, but even as a child he was always singing. His parents always knew when he was up in the morning because he would go around the house singing and humming. By the time he was sixteen, he knew two hundred songs by heart. He was an impressively large man for his day, standing a tall 6'4" and weighing 300 pounds.

Phillips early education began in a private school at age four in 1840. He progressed to Adams public grammar school, and then in 1847 began classes at the Boston Latin School. In 1851, he went on to study at Harvard from where he graduated in 1855. He tried teaching Latin at the Boston Latin School for six months without success, so he resigned his position. His minister, A.N. Vinton, advised Phillips to study theology at the Episcopal Divinity School in Alexandria, Virginia, which he did. He was ordained a deacon from there on July 1, 1859 and a week later he became rector of the 'Church of the Advent' in Philadelphia, where he was ordained a priest on Whitsunday in 1860. On January 1, 1862 he took the pulpit at the 'Church of the Holy Trinity' in Philadelphia, and then in 1869 he became rector of the 'Trinity Church' in Boston, where he served until 1891.

Three of his younger brothers, Frederic, Arthur and John all entered the ministry and became preachers of distinction in Cleveland, New York, and Springfield. During the Civil War, while at Holy Trinity, Brooks was known to be a staunch abolitionist and supported the Union cause. In May of 1865, Phillips was called upon to give, what turned out to be, a very memorable message about the assassinated president, Abraham Lincoln, whom he loved and admired. In 1880, he became the first American to preach before a member of the English Royal Family (Queen Victoria.) The last fifteen months of his life he served as the Bishop of Massachusetts. He was elected to the American Hall of Fame in 1910.

Phillips was noted for his "low church" views, and preached in churches of other denominations than his own. His sermons reflected a deep understanding and genuine sympathy with men of different views. He turned down other calls for his service, such as becoming a chaplain and professor at Harvard in 1881, and in 1886 he rejected a call to the office of assistant bishop of Pennsylvania in order to remain at his Boston parish, where he enjoyed working with youth, even though he remained a bachelor all of his life. Phillips was beloved by his congregation, especially the children, who found in their pastor a warm, open-hearted man who made religion something they could feel, understand, and practice in their everyday lives.

It is said that he had an irresistible personality, a sharp mind and a sunny nature. He brought to life Bible passages through the use of metaphors and gave Biblical teachings meaning for people of his own time. It seems that most of all he wanted to bring his passionate faith to all the people he met and impart to them that Christianity was the single most powerful force in the world, a force, which was able to transform individual lives. As one result of his Christian conviction, he spent a great deal of time with Harvard students, seeking to strengthen their Christian beliefs. Phillips was noted for his rapid style delivery of sermons, estimated at 250 words per minute, at his Protestant Episcopal Church. In 1878, his first volume of sermons sold more than two hundred thousand copies. Even in his day he was known as the "Prince of the Pulpit" and is now considered by many as "the greatest American preacher of the 19th century."

The Civil War years had taken a toll on Phillips. He was saddened among other things, by the fact that many of his own congregation had lost loved ones in the war. His own brother, George, had died from typhoid fever while serving in the Union army. Phillips needed a break to refresh his mind, body and soul, so he took a leave from his church and traveled to the Holy Land during Christmastime in 1865. The trip proved successful in renewing his spirit. Three years after his inspirational sabbatical experience in the Holy Land, Phillips said the memory of standing on the hills of Palestine looking down over Bethlehem was "still singing in my soul" and so he sat down with his pen and wrote the words to "O Little Town of Bethlehem" in 1868 for his Sunday school class of 36 kids to sing at a Sunday school church program.

Phillips also authored other lesser-known Christmas songs titled "Everywhere, Everywhere, Christmas Tonight" and "The Sky Can Still Remember." Phillips is known to have written some songs on his voyage to Japan in 1889, and these other Christmas songs may be from that time period, however, the exact dates of composition are unknown.

When he died in 1893 from diphtheria, a five-year old Boston girl paid him a high tribute by telling her mother "how happy the angels will be!" Today, a statue in tribute to Phillips Brooks stands outside the Trinity Church in Boston. The Phillips Brooks House was established at Harvard college in 1900 in honor of the work Phillips did with the students at Harvard.

We could certainly use more men like Phillips Brooks to be a positive example for our youth today.

JOHN BAPTISTE CALKIN

Composer of music for "I Heard The Bells On Christmas Day" in 1872

Born on March 16, 1827 in Middlesex,
London, England
Died on May 15, 1905 in Middlesex,
London, England

John Calkin was one of eight children born to James and Victoire (Tenniel) Calkin. On November 4, 1827 he was baptized at St. Pancras. Music came naturally to John, as he was reared in an English family of noted musicians who were mostly instrumentalists. His grandparents, Joseph and Mary Calkin, had two sons and three grandsons who became accomplished musicians, but it was John who became the most famous of all. The Calkin family roots can be traced back to Nathaniel Calkin who lived in 17th century Stafford, England.

John first studied music under his talented father who was a professional musician at a theatre and played multiple instruments. In 1846, at the age of 19, John was appointed organist and choirmaster at St. Columba College in Dublin, Ireland, which had been founded in 1843. Then, from 1853-63 he was the organist and choirmaster at Woburn Chapel in London. It was during this time period that he married Mary (Eurgain Edwards) in St. Pancras in 1857 and they went on to have three children, Annie, Edith and John, born in 1859, 1861 and 1862 respectively. Beginning in 1864, John served as the organist at the Camden Road Chapel for five years, and then he became organist at the St. Thomas Church in Camden Town from 1870-84.

In 1883, he further put his musical talent to work by becoming a professor at the Guildhall School of Music. John held other positions as well, including a position on the council of Trinity College in London. He was elected a fellow at the College of Organists, served as a professor at Croydon Conservatory, and he was a member of the Philharmonic Society. When not busy with his other commitments, John managed to compose multiple hymn tunes, service music, anthems, songs, and organ music.

John composed the hymn tune "Waltham" used with "I Heard The Bells On Christmas Day" in 1872. It was originally used for the hymn "Fling Out the Banner! Let It Float." This tune was first published in 'The Hymnary' collection of music in 1872. The tune is known for its 'martial swing' and the ease with which it can be sung. Who actually paired the poem by Longfellow with the tune "Waltham" remains a mystery, although it could have easily been John himself.

According to an 1881 census, John was prosperous enough in his music career to have the luxury of two live-in servants, Rose Weller, the cook, and Ruth Burgess, the housemaid, in addition to his wife, Mary, and their two children, while living on St. Augustines Road in St. Pancras. By the time of the 1901 census, Mary had died and John was living with his sister-in-law, Ruth Edwards, and his daughter, Annie, at 37 Hornsey Rise Gardens. John died at his Hornsey Rise Gardens home in London in 1905. He left most of his estate to his daughter, Annie, as designated in his last will and testament dated February 5, 1901. His son, John Sidney, received his father's 'plain gold ring' and his grandson, Clifford Sidney Calkin, was bequeathed John's gold watch and chain. John was dedicated to two things in his life...his family and music.

PLACIDE CAPPEAU

Author of "O Holy Night" in 1847

Born on October 25, 1808 in Roquemaure, France
Died on August 8, 1877 in Roquemaure, France

The village of Roquemaure, the lifelong home of Placide Cappeau, once had a castle where Pope Clement V died on April 20, 1314. In the 14th century, Roquemaure was the most important port on the right bank of the Rhone River. The Consuls of Roquemaure devised a very early policy for the production of wines, especially white wines, with the implementation of a system of strict regulations at the origin of the wine brand name 'Cotes du Rhone.'

The collegiate church in Roquemaure is dedicated to the patron saints of winegrowing and barrel making of the 'Cote du Rhone' region. This church contains an organ constructed in 1690, which was used by Emilie Laurey to perform "O Holy Night" for the first time on December 24, 1847, at the Midnight Mass. The text by Placide, a part-time poet, was reportedly written on December 3, 1847, about halfway on a long coach ride to Paris. Once in Paris, Placide presented his poem to the composer, Adolphe Adam,

through a mutual acquaintance with the Laurey family from Paris. Placide's main profession was, not surprisingly, a commissionaire of wines in the city of Roquemaure, which, as mentioned, was famous for its wine. He was evidently thought of well enough in his hometown to be elected to a term as mayor.

The original French title of Placide's poem was 'Minuit Chretiens' meaning 'Midnight, Christians.' The original title of the hymn "O Holy Night" was the very Christmas sounding name of "Cantique de Noel." Only recently, in America, has Placide begun to receive deserved recognition as the author of this song. In many music books, Adolphe Adam has erroneously received full credit as author and composer of this famous French Christmas hymn.

Late in his life Placide rejected Christianity and embraced socialistic free thought. He was also known to oppose inequality, slavery, injustice and oppression, which were pretty controversial viewpoints in his day, but to me, it sounds like he should have been admired for his viewpoints, instead of condemned. However, his rejection of Christianity was largely the reason why his hymn temporarily fell out of favor in some regional French churches in the late 19th century and early 20th century. Church authorities frowned on Placide turning his back on Christianity and in turn the church officials took their negative opinion of Placide out on his song, with one French bishop going so far as to denounce it for its "lack of musical taste and total absence of the spirit of religion." Obviously, Placide was not held in high esteem by the French church of his day, however, the popularity of "O Holy Night" was restored with the passage of time, and it is now noted for its beautiful words and melody, and is one of the most popular songs for singing as a solo during the Christmas season.

Placide was the son of Mathieu and Agathe Louise (Martinet) Cappeau, owners of a family vineyard business. When Placide was a boy of seven, Napoleon Bonaparte, the French Emperor, was defeated at the 'Battle of Waterloo.' The following year, Placide forever lost the use of his right hand in an accident. He had been playing with a friend, and they were handling a firearm, when the weapon discharged and struck Placide in the right hand. Napoleon died in

1821, when Placide was thirteen, and the population of France was 30 million.

The loss of his right hand did not prevent Placide from earning a first place in drawing from the Royal College of Avignon in 1825. In 1830, the Frenchman, Louis Braille, invented the alphabet for the blind that bears his name. After additional educational studies in Nimes and Paris, Placide earned a college degree in 1831, after which he became a wine seller. Placide was 31 when the Frenchman, Louis Daguerre, pioneered the invention of photography in 1839.

Placide became rather eccentric late in his life, as indicated by his request to be buried 'standing up.'

Placide is a classic example of how any person can do just one thing in their life, such as writing a poem, and as a result, achieve everlasting fame. It's rather ironic that he died in 1877, the same year that Thomas Edison invented the phonograph, the very instrument, which would play Placide's famous Christmas hymn...performed by a multitude of artists...over and over and over again in the years to come. In fact, in 1906, "O Holy Night" became the very first song broadcast via radio waves, when Reginald Fessenden, the former chief chemist for Thomas Edison, picked up his violin and played the song, shortly after he became the first man to speak over the airwaves, and moments before "O Holy Night" made history once again.

The Coming of Father Christmas.

By

E.F.Manning.

London
FREDERICK WARNE & C.º

JAMES CHADWICK

Translator of "Angels We Have Heard On High" in 1860

Born on April 24, 1813 in Drogheda, Ireland
Died on May 14, 1882 in Newcastle-upon-Tyne

James was one of eleven children born to John and Frances (Dromgoole) Chadwick, prosperous owners of a flax mill and linen manufacturing business. His father was English and his mother was Irish. His father John was imprisoned at one point for his religious stand of siding with Prince Charles and the Stuarts in 1745, and the family of Frances was persecuted for being Catholic. The Chadwick's played an active role in their local Catholic church and they funded a new Augustinian Church in Drogheda.

James was educated at Ushaw College until his ordination as a priest on December 17, 1836. He served as general prefect at the college for three years and then was appointed professor of philosophy for the next five years. He continued to teach humanities, mental philosophy, and pastoral theology until the year 1850 at which time he became Vice-President of the college. Due to health problems, he left Ushaw for a period of six years, before resuming his professor duties at Ushaw in 1856.

From 1859 to 1863 he served as chaplain to Lord Stourton before being elected the second Roman Catholic Bishop of the Hexhem and Newcastle diocese in 1866, where he headed that diocese for the next 16 years. James also served as the president of Ushaw College for one year in 1877.

During his time as a chaplain in 1860 he translated the 18th century French song 'Los Anges dans nos Campagnes' into English. His lyrics we know today are not a direct translation of the French words, but contain loose similarities to the French version. Chadwick's English version of the hymn, 'Angels We Have Heard On High', first appeared in 'Holy Family Hymns' in 1860.

Sources indicate the French version of the hymn was first published in Quebec in 1842.

It is stated that as a college professor he gained the esteem, respect, and affection of all his students. It is also said he was a man of great personal dignity and charm, who was remembered for his meekness and sweetness of manner.

Today he is best remembered for his English translation of the French Christmas hymn.

James passed away at his residence in Ryehill, Newcastle at 3 a.m. on May 14, 1882.

WILLIAM HAYMAN CUMMINGS

Arranger of "Hark! The Herald Angels Sing" in 1855

Born on August 22, 1831 in Sidbury,
Devonshire, England
Died on June 6, 1915 in London, England

William was the son of Edward Manley Cummings, a father who encouraged his son's singing and helped William get placed at a young age as a choirboy at St. Paul's Cathedral. After graduating from the University of London, William went on to become a celebrated tenor singer in England and America. William made two concert tours in America, singing tenor in primarily oratorios, with his last tour of America taking place in 1871. At the age of sixteen, he sang in the premiere performance of Mendelssohn's famous 'Elijah' oratorio on April 16, 1847, with Mendelssohn himself conducting. He was also noted for his impressive rendering of the tenor solos in Bach's "St. Matthew's Passion."

William married Clara Ann Hobbs in 1854 and they had ten children together.

In 1864 he sang at the Birmingham Festival, and afterwards became a familiar figure at similar events. In 1873 William composed the noted cantata 'The Fairy Ring.' He was instrumental in the founding of the Purcell Society, and wrote Henry Purcell's biography in 1882. He was also known to compose church music, glees and part songs. William served as professor of singing at the Royal Academy of Music from 1879-96, and at the same time, served as conductor of the Sacred Harmonic Society from 1882-88. Also, he was the principal of the Guildhall School of Music from 1896-1910, and an organist at Waltham Abbey in England, beginning in 1847. He held executive positions in the Philharmonic Society, the Musical Association, and the Incorporated Society of Musicians. His musical scholarship was demonstrated in his 'Primer of the Rudiments of Music' in 1877, and a 'Biographical Dictionary of Musicians' in 1892. In 1900 the University of Dublin conferred a Doctor of Music degree upon him.

It was during the time that William was organist at Waltham Abbey that he made the hymn setting for "Hark! The Herald Angels Sing" in 1855, a full 116 years after Charles Wesley penned the lyrics. He adapted a theme from the second movement of Mendelssohn's "Festgesang" from 1840, which was a cantata to commemorate the invention of the printing press. William took part of the section, 'God Is Light', which he considered 'a noble and spirited choral' and fitted it to Wesley's words. William's choir sang his newly created Christmas hymn on Christmas Day, and it was first published with the tune of 'Mendelssohn' in Richard R. Chopes' 1857 collection titled 'Congregational Hymn and Tune Book.' The hymn became one of the most popular carols within a decade of William's arrangement being published.

Not much is known about William's family or early life, but by the time of William's death in 1915 he had put together a personal library of 4,500 volumes, which were dispersed at auction a few years later. William is another example of a talented musician who accomplished so much during his life, and yet is remembered primarily for his contribution to one of our favorite traditional Christmas hymns. I feel this is a testimonial to the powerful influence of Christmas music on our world.

WILLIAM CHATTERTON DIX

Author of "What Child Is This?" in 1865
Author of "As With Gladness Men of Old" in 1858

Born on June 14, 1837 in Bristol, England
Died on September 9, 1898 at Cheddar
in Somerset, England

William Dix was the son of John and Sussanah (Moore) Dix, his father being a medical doctor in Bristol, England. John Dix had written a biography of the poet, Thomas Chatterton, and it was in the poet's honor that William received his middle name. Obviously, some of Chatterton's poetic talent rubbed off on William. It's interesting to note that Queen Victoria of England began her reign the year that William was born and she remained the Queen of England throughout William's lifetime. When William was six years old the British novelist, Charles Dickens, wrote "A Christmas Carol" and a year later, George Williams of London, England, founded the Y.M.C.A. organization.

William was educated at the Bristol Grammar School and trained to become a merchant. In 1863, William became a manager of an English marine insurance company in Glasgow, Scotland and eventually went on to own a very successful insurance business of his own. After settling into the insurance business, William married a lady by the name of Juliet (Wartnaby) in 1864 and they went on to have seven children together during a thirteen-year period from 1868 to1881. The insurance business became William's lifelong occupation, and the study of languages and the writing of poetry, were merely avocations for him. One of his contemporaries said of William "that few modern writers have shown so signal (special) a gift as his for the difficult art of hymn writing."

William was a talented poet and many of his 40 original hymns were published in his own collections 'Hymns of Love and Joy' in 1861, and 'Altar Songs, Verses on the Holy Eucharist' of 1878. Several of his hymns are translations from the Greek and Ethiopian languages. William wrote "As With Gladness Men of Old" one evening during Epiphany of 1858, while convalescing from an illness. This hymn was included in his 'Hymns of Love and Joy' of 1861 with music by Conrad Kocher, which had been adapted by William Monk. The hymn tells the Epiphany story, and is based upon the Gospel text in Matthew 2:9-11. The original poem text was slightly revised with Dix's approval and the revised version was published in 'Hymns Ancient & Modern' in 1875. It's interesting to note that Dix did not like Kocher's tune, but he decided that since the song had already been published with the words and music joined together, it was too late to change it. Dix stated, "I dislike it, but now nothing will displace it." Perhaps it was for the best in the long run that the tune was not displaced, because at one time in the late 19th century the hymn was considered to be one of "the best one hundred hymns in the English language." In 1865, William published 'The Manger Throne' poem from which three stanzas were taken and fitted to the tune of "Greensleeves" by John Stainer in 1871, creating the Christmas hymn "What Child Is This?" It was published in Stainer's hymn collection "Christmas Carols, New and Old" in 1871. This was the first major English language carol collection, and did much to promote carols of all types. With Dix's Christmas poem included in this collection, "What Child Is This?" received some excellent publicity right from the start...thanks to Sir John Stainer.

JOHN SULLIVAN DWIGHT

English Translator of "O Holy Night" in 1855

Born on May 13, 1813 in Boston, Massachusetts
Died on September 5, 1893 in Boston, Massachusetts

John Sullivan Dwight was the son of John and Mary (Corey) Dwight, and a graduate of Harvard University in 1832. John prepared for the Unitarian ministry by attending the Harvard Divinity School from where he graduated in 1836. For the next four years his career was sidetracked by his interest and involvement in the 'Transcendentalist Movement.' He was finally ordained a minister in a Unitarian church in Northampton, Massachusetts in 1840, but within a year left the ministry, because he was constantly stricken with panic attacks when he faced crowds of people and he would then become physically ill as a result. In 1841, he saw a more promising future when George and Sophia Ripley founded the Brook Farm commune "to prepare a society of liberal, intelligent, and cultivated persons, whose relations with each other would permit a more simple and wholesome life, than can be led amidst the pressure of our competitive institutions."

John served as director of the Brook Farm School where he taught music and Latin, and organized musical and theatrical events. He was a student of classical music, especially by Beethoven, and he was largely responsible for establishing Beethoven's reputation in America. John is considered to be the first American classical music critic of note. The Brook Farm way of life ended in 1847, the result of debt and dissension, and this was a big disappointment to John. However, it turned out to be fortunate for us, because after this turn of events, John moved back to Boston and began his career in musical journalism. On February 12, 1851, after a courtship of several years, John married a former Brook Farm resident, Mary Bullard, who was known as the 'Nightingale' for her beautiful singing voice. John then founded "Dwight's Journal of Music" in 1852, which became the most influential musical publication of 19th century America. His journal was published from 1852-81.

John made his only trip to Europe in July of 1860, but the experience was marred by the death of his wife at home in Boston, on September 6. The news did not reach John until October, and although he was shocked by the news, he decided to continue his travels for another year before returning to Boston in November of 1861 to resume his work as the editor of his journal.

The success of his journal over the years was tied into the musical developments around the Boston area. The Music Hall was built in 1852, the Harvard Musical Association began its sponsorship of concerts in 1866, and the Boston Conservatory of Music and the New England Conservatory of Music were both founded in 1867. John was also instrumental in organizing the Boston Philharmonic Society in 1865 and the professorship of music at Harvard in 1876.

John published his English translation of "O Holy Night" in 1855, while he was the editor of "Dwight's Journal of Music." He had read the French version of the Christmas hymn "Cantique de Noel" during his journal studies and decided it needed to be introduced to America in the English language. He was right... and we are grateful.

HENRY JOHN GAUNTLETT

Composer of music for "Once In Royal David's City" in 1849

Born on July 9, 1805 in Wellington, Shropshire, England
Died on February 21, 1876 in London, England

Henry was the fourth of twelve children, and the oldest son, born to his father who was also named Henry and Arabella (Jenkinson Davies). His father was the Curate at the Wellington Parish Church when the younger Henry was born. In 1814, the family moved to Olney, where at the age of only nine years old, Henry became the church organist after taking six months of lessons from his mother. Although being a gifted organist, Henry the elder discouraged his son from being a professional musician. Therefore, Henry instead became a lawyer and practiced in London for 15 years until he was 39 years old, when he abandoned law for a music career.

In 1827, Henry took his first post as an organist at St. Olave, Southwark and remained in that position until 1846. In that position he began to campaign for the reform of organ design. His design ideas led to the extending of the pedal compass and patenting an electrical apparatus to power the organ in 1852. His collaboration with organ designer, William Hill, lasted from the 1830's to 1860.

Henry married Henrietta Gipps in 1841.

Gauntlett edited 'The Musical World' and later provided articles for various publications. Henry was also in much demand as a performer. In 1846, Mendelssohn chose him to play the organ part in Mendelssohn's first performance of 'Elijah'

It was in 1849 when Henry composed the music titled 'Irby' for the song lyrics written by Cecil Frances Alexander the year before. Despite their collaboration on the hymn 'Once In Royal David's City' the two never had the opportunity to meet in person.

The Christmas hymn was first published in a song collection titled 'Christmas Carols' in 1849.

Henry was a prolific hymn writer of several pieces of church music. His contributions to organ design, Gregorian music, and congregational song, ranks him as an important figure in English Victorian church music. He was given the title of 'The Father of Church Music' because he was the creator of the school of four-part hymn tunes.

Felix Mendelssohn wrote of him in 1844, "His literary attainments, his knowledge of the history of music, his acquaintance with acoustical law, his marvelous memory, and his philosophical turn of mind as well as practical experience, render him one of the most remarkable professors of the age. I know but very few of his countrymen or mine whose masterly performance on the organ, whose skill in writing, and whose perfect knowledge of musical literature of ancient and modern times may be compared to his."

Henry died at his home in Kensington in 1876, survived by his wife and six children.

FRANZ XAVER GRUBER

Composer of music for "Silent Night" in 1818

Born on November 25, 1787 in Hochburg,
Upper Austria
Died on June 7, 1863 in Hallein, Germany

Franz Gruber was the fourth son of a linen weaver, Josephus Gruber, who wanted his boy to stay in the trade, but fortunately for us...that didn't happen. The mother of Franz was Anna (Danner) Gruber. Franz began to study the organ in 1805 with Georg Hartdobler, the organist at Burghausen. He graduated from high school in the town of Ried, in 1806. From 1807-29 he taught school at Arnsdorf, and on July 6, 1807 Franz married Elisabeth Fischinger in that same village. Beginning in 1816 he supplemented his income by serving as the organist at the Roman Catholic parish of St. Nicholas Church in nearby Oberndorf. He was living in an apartment over the schoolhouse in Arnsdorf when Joseph Mohr brought him the poem of "Stille Nacht" and requested that Franz put some music to it. On August 25, 1825 Elisabeth Gruber died and Franz married Maria Breitfuss on January 24, 1826. After 1833, he was the headmaster at Berndorf and organist at Hallein.

His son, Felix, succeeded him at Hallein. Franz's wife, Maria, died on April 26, 1841 and Katharina Wimmer became his third wife on January 25, 1842.

Franz wrote more than 90 compositions, but is remembered only for "Stille Nacht."
He composed the music for "Silent Night" on Christmas Eve in 1818. He set the music for two solo voices, chorus, and guitar accompaniment. The guitar accompaniment was needed because the church organ had broken down. Within a few hours Gruber composed the simple melody that generations of people have loved ever since, and the song was sung that same evening in the St. Nicholas Church. The song was obtained and carried outside of Oberndorf and subsequently 'promoted' by an organ repairman, Karl Mauracher (1789-1844), and between 1831-41 was sang in various places by Austrian singing groups such as the Strassers and the Rainers. The hymn was published in Germany and the United States during the 1830's and 1840's, but the author and composer remained unknown. It wasn't until 1854 that the world learned the names of Gruber and Mohr. Until that time the song had circulated with anonymous credit, but that year the King of Prussia, Frederick Wilhelm IV, first heard the song and instructed his royal court musicians in Berlin to find out the names of the author and composer. They inquired with monks at the St. Peter's monastery in Salzburg about the song's origin. It was Felix, Franz's son, who convinced them that the credit should go to his father and Joseph Mohr. In 1995 a long lost arrangement of "Stille Nacht" written by the hand of Joseph Mohr was authenticated. In the upper right hand corner of the arrangement Mohr had written 'Melodie von Fr. Xav. Gruber.' The original guitar arrangement is yet to be found, but five other Gruber manuscripts of the carol exist.

Franz's former home in Hallein is now the site of the 'Franz Xaver Gruber Museum.' It contains several rooms filled with furnishings from his period, along with exhibits dealing with the history of "Silent Night." Gruber's grave is located outside the home. I guess you could say that Franz did not travel far in his life, for he died only about twelve miles from where he was born, but the Christmas hymn he created has traveled as far as a song can go.

BENJAMIN RUSSELL HANBY

Author & Composer of "Up On The Housetop" in 1864
Author & Composer of "Who Is He In Yonder Stall"
in 1866

Born on July 22, 1833 in Rushville, Ohio
Died on March 16, 1867 in Chicago, Illinois

Benjamin Hanby was one of eight children born to William and Ann (Miller) Hanby. To understand Benjamin's songwriting roots better, it is necessary to present some background information on his father. William had moved to Ohio as a young man where he found work as a saddler before pursuing a career in the ministry. In 1845, William became a bishop in the United Brethren Church, and he used his position to advocate social reform causes, including abolitionism. His homes in Rushville and Westerville, Ohio served as stations for the Underground Railroad. William co-founded Otterbein College in Westerville, Ohio in 1847, and then purchased a home in Westerville in 1854, which today has been converted into a museum known as the "Hanby House." The house contains period furnishings and many personal items that belonged to the Hanby family, including a large collection of sheet music and songs. Among them are the original plates for the first edition of the song "Darling Nelly Gray," which Benjamin wrote in 1856.

Benjamin began writing songs while he was a student at Otterbein, and obviously his writing was influenced by his father's participation in the Underground Railroad for helping black slaves escape from slave states to Free states. His "Darling Nelly Gray" song did much to arouse sympathy for America's slaves. He based his song on the life of Joseph Selby, a Kentucky slave who was helped by Benjamin's father, but who had lost his bride-to-be, Nellie, when she was sold into slavery in Georgia.

Benjamin graduated from Otterbein in 1858 and married Mary Kate Winter in June of that year. Three years later he became a pastor in the United Brethren Church at Lewisburg, Ohio from 1861 to 1863. He then went to work for the John Church Music Company in Cincinnati for one year. He wrote 'Up on the Housetop' at New Paris, Ohio in 1864, while a minister at a church there.

In 1865, he joined the staff at the Root & Cady Music Company of Chicago and was still employed there at the time of his death. While working at the Root & Cady Company, Benjamin compiled a collection of songs titled "Our Song Birds" which included 60 of his tunes. Hanby's best known Christmas songs "Up on the House Top" and "Who Is He in Yonder Stall" were both published in 1866. "Up on the House Top" first appeared under the original title "Santa Claus." This song was most likely influenced by Clement Clarke Moore's poem "A Visit from St. Nicholas" written in 1822. As with most children since the 1820's, Hanby would have been well acquainted with Moore's poem. No one before Moore had suggested that Santa's sleigh could land on a rooftop, which inspired the first verse of Hanby's song.

Benjamin's sister, Amanda, became well known in her own right as the first woman foreign missionary in the United Brethren Church when she was commissioned for service in Sierra Leone, Africa, in 1862. Many of the Hanby family, including Benjamin, are buried in the Otterbein Cemetery in Westerville, Ohio.

GEORGE FREDERIC HANDEL

Composer of music for "While Shepherds Watched Their Flocks by Night" in 1728

Born on February 23, 1685 in Halle, Germany
Died on April 14, 1759 in London, England

George Handel was the son of a prosperous barber-surgeon, Georg Handel, and Dorothea (Taust). His father dreamed of his son becoming a lawyer. His father did not regard music as a suitable profession for a young man of the middle class and he did not do very much to advance his son's musical talents, except that at the age of eight his father consented to letting George take organ lessons. George soon learned the basics of composing and mastered the playing of the organ, violin and oboe.

In 1702 George entered the University of Halle to study law, but after the death of his father, he was free to focus on a career in music. He traveled to Hamburg where he became a second violinist in the orchestra at an opera house and later wrote his first opera there. Beginning in 1706, George studied opera for three years in Italy before being appointed the conductor to the Elector of Hanover in 1710. In that same year, George visited London for the first time, the city he would later call

home for nearly fifty years. Beginning in 1718 he served as a chapel master, until the Royal Academy of Music was founded in 1720 and George was appointed one of the musical directors there. It was in the next twenty years that he experienced his greatest fame. During this time George became a naturalized English citizen, in 1727, and he focused on composing operas and oratorios. In 1737, he suffered a stroke of paralysis and was physically debilitated for several months, but he recovered fully and returned to composing. His multiple compositions from 1742-52 primarily focused on biblical subjects, but when his eyesight failed him in 1753, he had to collaborate with friends on compositions from that time forward.

George was blind for the last seven years of his life, but he continued to conduct oratorio performances. He had just completed directing a performance of "Messiah" in London on April 6, 1759 when he fainted and was helped home to bed. He never recovered and died eight days later at the age of 74. George was blessed by having a mother, the daughter of a Lutheran clergyman, who was intimately acquainted with the Bible. The influence of her teaching on her son is evidenced by his "resolve to die a member of the communion, in which, he had been born and bred." He was buried with honors in Westminster Abbey on April 20. His total compositions include 46 operas, 32 oratorios, multiple cantatas, chamber duets, church and instrumental music.

George is perhaps best known for his oratorio "Messiah" composed in the brief span of 23 days, but in 1728 he had written an opera "Siroe, Re di Persia" from which a tune was taken and applied to the Christmas hymn "While Shepherds Watched Their Flocks By Night" in 1861. His second connection to Christmas music comes from the fact that, allegedly, Lowell Mason utilized a small portion of George's "Messiah" music for his 1839 arrangement of "Joy To The World," but this fact has never been confirmed.

George is best remembered for his contributions to classical music, but I'm glad his music contributed a 'touch of class' to at least one of our favorite Christmas hymns.

Thank you, George Handel, for the musical legacy you left generations of us to enjoy.

KARL POMEROY HARRINGTON

*Composer of music for "There's A Song In The Air"
in 1904*

Born on June 13, 1861 in Somersworth,
New Hampshire
Died on November 14, 1953 in Middletown,
Connecticut

Karl was the son of Calvin and Eliza (Chase) Harrington. Calvin was a Latin professor who hailed from Vermont and Eliza was born in New Hampshire. Karl lived at home through his college days and graduated from Wesleyan University in Middletown, Connecticut in 1882, from where he received his M.A. in 1885. While attending Wesleyan from 1882-85 he taught high school in Westfield, Massachusetts. After earning his masters degree he taught Latin at Wesleyan Academy in Wilbraham, Massachusetts from 1885-87. For the next two years Karl went to Germany and studied in Berlin before returning to America for a couple more years of study at Yale. During his time at Yale he tutored students in Latin at Wesleyan University. Karl became a Latin professor at the University of North Carolina and served there from 1891-99 before moving on to Maine University to teach Latin from 1899-1905. Karl returned to his alma mater of Wesleyan to teach Latin from 1905-29. At the same time that Karl was pursuing his professional academic career, he became an accomplished musician and served as an organist and choir director in various Methodist churches, including those at Stamford and Hartford, Connecticut. While in Maine, Karl served as president and director of the Festival Chorus in Bangor. Somehow, Karl managed to find time to be a member of 'The Hymn Society' of New York, and to author numerous books on classical and musical topics.

Karl married Jennie Eliza Canfield on November 25, 1886 during the period of time he taught Latin at Wesleyan Academy and they went on to have three children together.

Karl wrote the hymn tune 'Christmas Song' for "There's A Song In The Air" in 1904 while staying at his summer home in New Hampshire. The song was created on a hot summer's day, after Karl had read Josiah Holland's poem in an 1879 edition of 'Complete Poetical Writings' by Holland. It had been 32 years since Holland had penned the words for this Christmas hymn, but Karl felt that the poem needed to be put to music for all to enjoy.

Karl was serving as the co-editor of the 1905 Methodist Hymnal when this hymn was first printed with his tune in that hymnal. Actually, three composers submitted tunes for use with Holland's words, and all three were printed in the 1905 Methodist Hymnal, however, Karl's composition became the favorite with the passage of time. Karl contributed twelve tunes to the 1905 hymnal, but it's the 'Christmas Song' tune for which we remember him today.

Let's stop for a moment and consider everything that Karl experienced during his full life of 92 years. He was born at the start of the Civil War and died the year that the Korean War ended. His life spanned an exciting period of progress that went from the Pony Express days to the production of atomic-powered submarines. Abraham Lincoln was president when Karl was born and Dwight Eisenhower was president at his death.

THOMAS HELMORE

Arranger of "Good King Wenceslas" in 1853
Arranger of "O Come, O Come Emmanuel" in 1854

Born on May 7, 1811 in Kidderminster, England
Died on July 6, 1890 in London, England

Thomas Helmore was the son of a Congregationalist minister, Thomas, and Olive (Holloway) Helmore. At age nine his family moved from Kidderminster to Stratford-upon-Avon, and he was educated at Mill Hill School until the age of 16. Thomas was then trained as an English teacher and choir trainer in his father's church.

Queen Victoria had just begun her 63-year reign the year that Thomas began his higher education at Magdalen Hall at Oxford University in 1837. In 1840, he graduated from Oxford and was ordained a Congregational minister.

He served as curate and then vicar at Lichfield Cathedral from 1840 to 1842, before moving on to St. Mark's College in Chelsea, England, in 1842, where he remained for nearly four decades. St. Mark's was a new institution, founded in 1841, at the time that Thomas began his service there, and it was established for the training of teachers in church schools. It was here that Thomas's love of music was cultivated as he taught his students there to sing daily choral services.

On January 11, 1844, Thomas married Kate Wilson Pridham and they had seven children together by the names of Arthur, Thomas, Walter, Frederick, Katherine, Margaret and Sarah. Thomas received his Master of Arts degree from Oxford in 1845, and the following year he became 'master of the choristers' of the Chapel Royal at St. Mark's.

During the year 1854, while in his position as 'master of the children', Thomas auditioned eleven-year old Arthur Seymour Sullivan who desired a place in the boy's choir. The future famous composer impressed Thomas with his singing ability. "His voice was very sweet and his style of singing far more sympathetic than that of most boys" recorded Thomas.

It was during the time that Thomas was serving as precentor (choir leader) of St. Mark's College that he created the musical setting and harmony for "Good King Wenceslas," which had been written by his friend and collaborator, John Mason Neale, in 1853. That same year, Thomas' arrangement was published in the carol collection titled 'Carols for Christmas.' As the musical editor of Neale's translations of Latin hymns, Thomas played a key role in the restoration of plainsong to English church services. He believed in using plainsong for congregational singing, and he was considered an authority on the subject in Anglican circles. It earned him the title 'The Pioneer of Gregorian Music.'

He had a hand in publishing multiple hymn collections from 1849 to 1881. Thomas's second lasting contribution to Christmas music was his 1854 adaptation of the "Veni Emmanuel" tune used for John Mason Neale's 1851 translation of "O Come, O Come Emmanuel." Neale and Helmore published their completed songs in a work called "Hymnal Noted" in 1854.

Thomas received a pension in 1877 for 35 years of service at St. Marks. He died peacefully in his residence at St. George's Square, London, in 1890, after suffering from bronchitis and a couple light strokes over the previous six years. Two sons, Arthur and Walter, who were involved in the English theater during the late 1800's and early 1900's, survived him.

Thanks to the collaboration between John Mason Neale and Thomas Helmore in the 1850's we are the beneficiaries of two favorite traditional Christmas songs that live 'on and on' from one year to the next.

Good King Wenceslas

JOSIAH GILBERT HOLLAND

Author of "There's A Song In The Air" in 1872

Born on July 24, 1819 in Belchertown, Massachusetts
Died on October 12, 1881 in New York, New York

Josiah Holland was the fourth of seven children born to Harrison and Anna (Gilbert) Holland. The Holland family ancestry in America is traced back to John and Judith Holland, Puritans who came from Plymouth, England to America in the 17th century. Harrison Holland was a hardworking, yet thriftless man, who held a series of jobs in a succession of western Massachusetts's towns and he also dabbled with inventions.

As a result of his father constantly moving the family, Josiah's early educational opportunities were limited, but eventually he managed to enter Northampton High School where he became a hardworking student. It does appear though that some of his father's restlessness rubbed off on Josiah, because early on he went through a string of jobs as a penmanship teacher, a maker of daguerreotypes, a copyist, and a district schoolmaster. At the age of twenty-one he turned to the study of medicine and was graduated from Berkshire Medical College, Pittsfield,

Massachusetts, in 1844. He practiced medicine in Springfield, Massachusetts for a short time, but developed a dislike for this profession. He married Elizabeth L. (Chapin) from Springfield on October 17, 1845, and they went on to have three children together. After ending his medical profession in 1847, Josiah dabbled with publishing an unsuccessful literary journal before establishing a teaching career in Richmond, Virginia, and Vicksburg, Mississippi. He enjoyed teaching as it gave him the feeling that he was serving his community and also provided him an outlet for his love of public speaking; nevertheless, at the age of thirty he resettled in Springfield and worked for the 'Republican' newspaper. His job there was to utilize his knowledge of ordinary people to provide 'human interest' material for a column in the paper. Using the pseudonym of Timothy Titcomb, he began a series of popular morality articles, which he referred to as "plain talks on familiar subjects." He exhibited remarkable aptitude for journalism and remained with the paper for fifteen years before selling his interest in the 'Republican' in 1866. Between 1868 and 1870 Josiah went to Europe and worked as a popular lecturer, before returning to America to co-found and edit the 'Scribner's Monthly' magazine beginning in 1870. He became a member of the board of education of New York City in 1872, and in 1873 briefly held the chairmanship of the board of trustees of New York College. By this time, he was a well-known editor and author, possessing both fame and wealth. He had sold more than a half million volumes of poetry, essays, and other writings. His primary message was morality and spirituality as the source of answers to life's problems.

Josiah authored many books from 1855 on, including 'The Marble Prophecy and Other Poems' in 1872, which included his popular Christmas poem we know as the hymn "There's A Song In The Air." This hymn has proved to be his gift and lasting legacy to the world. He died twenty-three years before Karl Harrington composed the music for this Christmas hymn in 1904. Josiah died suddenly and unexpectedly at home from a heart attack in 1881 at the age of 62.

JOHN HENRY HOPKINS, JR.

Author & Composer of "We Three Kings" 1857

Born on October 28, 1820 in Pittsburgh, Pennsylvania
Died on August 14, 1891 in Troy, New York

John Henry Hopkins, Jr. was one of thirteen children born to the Protestant Episcopal Bishop of Vermont, John Hopkins, Sr., who had come to America from Dublin, Ireland in 1801. His father was a talented man who was successful in a variety of work, including that of an ironmaster, schoolteacher, lawyer, priest and finally the second bishop of Vermont in 1865. His mother, Melusina (Muller) Hopkins, was of German descent and came from Hamburg, Germany. Not much is known of John's formative or teenage years. We begin our knowledge of John with the fact that he was educated at the University of Vermont and graduated from that educational institution in 1839.

After graduation, John taught for a time in a school established by his father, and for a time after that he studied law while working as a reporter in New York City. From 1842-44 he tutored children in Savannah, Georgia, before returning to Vermont University to earn his M.A. degree in 1845. In an attempt to create a fundraiser to help with family finances in 1846,

John and his father designed and printed drawing books of landscapes, figures and flowers. One book was titled the "Vermont Drawing Book of Flowers" and it demonstrated the artistic skill of the two men, but unfortunately, the books did not sell very well. So John entered the General Theological Seminary in New York City in 1847 and served as the music instructor there before graduating and being ordained a deacon in the Protestant Episcopal Church in 1850. In 1853, John founded the 'Church Journal' and was the proprietor and editor of that publication until May of 1868. During those years as editor of the 'Church Journal,' John applied his artistic talents in designing stained-glass windows, Episcopal seals, and a wide variety of other church ornaments. At the same time his musical talents led to the writing and composing of a number of fine hymns and tunes, as well as anthems and service pieces.

It was in 1857 that John authored and composed the Christmas hymn "We Three Kings" for a church Christmas pageant. John never married or had any children of his own, but his nieces and nephews loved his new song and it was first published in his "Carols, Hymns and Songs" collection of 1862. The hymn gained further popularity by being included in John Stainers' 1871 collection of carols titled "Christmas Carols New & Old." As a man who enjoyed keeping busy, John helped form Episcopal dioceses in Pittsburgh, Albany and Long Island from 1865 to 1868. He was ordained a priest in 1872, and in that same year he became the rector of Trinity Church in Plattsburg, New York. In 1876 he took a similar position at Christ Church in Williamsport, Pennsylvania, a post that he held until 1887. John authored many pamphlets and articles from 1866 to 1887 and penned other Christmas carols, including "Gather Around the Christmas Tree." Although John did not write great quantities of hymns, he is remembered as being one of the great leaders in the development of hymnody in the Episcopal Church during the 19th century. John died at a friend's home near Hudson, New York, on August 14, 1891. His biography entitled 'A Champion of the Cross' was published in 1894.

HENRY WADSWORTH LONGFELLOW

Author of "I Heard The Bells On Christmas Day"
in 1863

Born on February 27, 1807 in Portland, Maine
Died on March 24, 1882 in Cambridge, Massachusetts

Henry Longfellow was the son of Stephen and Zilpha (Wadsworth) Longfellow. His father was a lawyer and United States congressman, and his father's ancestor, William Longfellow, had emigrated from England to Massachusetts in 1676. Henry's mother was a descendant of the Mayflower pilgrims, John and Priscilla Alden.

As a boy, the War of 1812 made a lasting impression on Henry, because it had broken the peacefulness of his young life. At the age of fifteen he entered Bowdoin College at Brunswick, Maine, and graduated from that institution in 1825 with honors. He briefly entered his father's law office before being offered a professorship of modern languages at Bowdoin College. To prepare himself for this position he left for Europe in May of 1826 and spent three and a half years learning the languages of France, Italy, Spain, Germany, Holland and England. In late 1829 Henry returned to America and taught at Bowdoin for six years. During this time

he married Mary Story Potter on September 14, 1831, but just four years later, she died in Rotterdam while they were on a European trip.

Upon his return to America in December of 1836, Henry took up residence in Cambridge and began to teach modern languages at Harvard College. His first poems were published in 1839. On July 13, 1843 he was married for a second time, to Frances Elizabeth Appleton of Boston, and they had six children together. Poetry flowed from Henry's pen year after year until 1861, when two events cast a gloom on his life and for a time interrupted his poetic activity. First, the Civil War broke out and his oldest son Charles was seriously wounded in battle. Secondly, and most devastating to Henry, was the loss of his wife, who burned to death in their home when her dress caught fire from a candle, while she was trying to preserve some of her daughter Edith's hair clippings in wax. It was a long time before Henry recovered from the shock of the loss of his beloved 'Fanny', but by 1863 he was back writing poetry on a regular basis, and his writing continued the remainder of his life.

Henry penned the words to "I Heard The Bells On Christmas Day" on Christmas day in 1863. He was inspired to write the poem by the chiming church bells in the city, and he immediately presented the poem to the Sunday school of the Unitarian Church of the Disciples in Boston. His poem was originally titled "Christmas Bells" and was first published under that title in a collection of his poems entitled 'Flower de Luce' in 1867. The original poem contained two verses that referred specifically to the Civil War and these verses are seldom seen or heard today, but it's not surprising they were included in his poem, which was written a mere six months after the Battle of Gettysburg. The poem was made into a Christmas hymn when music by John Calkin was matched with the words sometime after Henry's death.

In the last years of his life Henry suffered from rheumatism, which left him "never free from pain." His health began to decline in early 1882 and he died from peritonitis on March 24th. He's remembered as the most influential American poet of his day.

MARTIN LUTHER

Author of "From Heaven Above" (Von Himmel Hoch) in 1534
Author of "To Shepherds As They Watched By Night" in 1543

Born on November 10, 1483 in Eisleben, Germany
Died on February 18, 1546 in Eisleben, Germany

Martin was the son of Hans and Margarethe (Lindemann) Luder. His father was a copper miner and the family was classified as peasants, but despite this lowly start in life, Martin received a full education at Magedburg, Eisenach and Erfurt. After graduation from the University of Erfurt with an M.A. in 1505, Martin entered the monastery for two years. He had intended to study law, but due to a narrow escape from death by lightning, he changed his mind and became an Augustinian monk. Martin became a priest in 1507 and then in 1508 he was appointed to the faculty of the University of Wittenberg where he lectured on moral theology and the Holy Scriptures. Martin spent the year of 1510 in Rome and was shocked at the corruption within the Catholic Church. In 1512 he received his Doctor of Divinity degree and he began to promote a more Biblical theology. It was on October 31, 1517 that he nailed the 95 theses (complaints) on the door of the Wittenberg Castle Church denouncing the abuses connected to the practice of selling indulgences to raise money for the church. It was after this that Martin was branded a heretic by the church and an outlaw by the state, but he continued to pursue reform in the church and broke away from the Catholic Church in 1521. Because of his efforts in church reform, the Bible was soon introduced into the homes of the German people in their own language, and Martin earned the title 'Father of the German Reformation.'

Martin had been a singer as a boy and studied music while a monk. He became a skilled hymn writer, and is credited with writing 37 hymns. He published his first hymnbook in 1524, and wrote his most famous hymn "A Mighty Fortress Is Our God" in 1529. His musical abilities, which included the playing of the flute and the lute, led to the introduction of hymns for congregational use. Martin gave music the highest and most honorable place after theology. He once wrote that "music is a gift and grace of God, not an invention of men…it makes people cheerful…then one forgets all wrath, impurity and other devices."

Martin's name was for a long time attached to the children's Christmas hymn "Away In A Manger," but there is no evidence that he wrote the lullaby and the music history books of today have set the record straight that "Away In A Manger" originated in America in the late 19th century. However, Martin did love Christmas and children, and he loved to join the children in celebrating Christmas. Special festivities were held for the children at Martin's home on Christmas Eve. "From Heaven Above" was a children's hymn written by Martin in 1534 and it was his custom to have a student, dressed as an angel, sing the first seven verses, and then have the children respond by singing the remaining eight verses, climaxed by a gleeful dance during the last verse. Martin wrote this hymn while sitting beside the cradle of his little son, Paul, and then joined the words to the tune of a popular German folksong. Martin was married in 1525 and had six children with his wife, Katharina von Bora, a former nun. He suffered from a variety of ill health from 1531 until his death from an apoplectic stroke and apparent heart attack in 1546.

LOWELL MASON

Arranger of "Joy to the World" in 1836

Born on January 8, 1792 in Medfield, Massachusetts
Died on August 11, 1872 in Orange, New Jersey

Lowell Mason was born into a family that was able to trace its ancestry back seven generations, when Robert Mason came to America from England with John Winthrop and the Puritans in 1630. Lowell was the oldest of five children born to Johnson and Catharine (Hartshorn) Mason. His siblings were named Lucretia, Johnson, Arnold, and Timothy. Lowell spent time as a youth working in his father's dry goods store. He was primarily a self-taught musician who in his own words "spent twenty years of his life in doing nothing save playing on all manner of musical instruments." Lowell could play the clarinet, violin, cello, flute, piano, and organ by the time he was twenty. His parents did not want him to become a musician, even though they both sang in their church choir for 30 years, but they encouraged Lowell's early fondness for music and saw to it that his talent was cultivated. He was so proficient in vocal music that at age sixteen he was appointed the leader of the village choir and a teacher of singing classes. With limited opportunities in Medfield, at the age of twenty, he moved to Savannah, Georgia and found work as a bank clerk, while continuing to practice, conduct, and teach music. In 1817, Lowell married Abigail Gregory in Massachusetts and they went on to be married nearly fifty-five years and to have four sons, Daniel, Lowell, William and Henry, who also made careers in the music business. While in Georgia, Lowell worked with F.L. Abel in putting together a collection of psalm tunes titled 'The Handel and Haydn Society's Collection of Church Music' in 1822. The book sold 50,000 copies, netting Lowell $30,000, but initially it did not have his name attached to it, because according to Lowell "I was then a bank officer in Savannah, and did not want to be known as a musical man, as I had not the least thought of ever making music a profession." The book led to a greater appreciation of music by the public in the New England states, so he returned to Boston in 1827 and took "general charge of music in the churches there."

Lowell was interested in the introduction of music into public schools, so he joined G.J. Webb in establishing the 'Boston Academy of Music' in 1833, which prescribed that music become a regular course of instruction in the public schools of Boston and subsequently throughout the entire country. Lowell was among the first to preach that children had a right to receive instruction in music at public expense, and he was the man who gained them that right. Beginning in 1834, Lowell started a series of yearly music conventions to train music teachers, and in 1836, he obtained the right to have music taught in all the schools of Boston. During this same period of time, he published a large number of manuals and collections, which sold well and provided him with financial wealth. One of his tune books 'Carmina Sacra' sold a half million copies from 1841 to 1860. In 1853, he co-founded the 'New York Normal Institute' with George F. Root and William B. Bradbury, for the purpose of training music teachers. New York University conferred the degree of 'Doctor of Music' upon Lowell in 1855. It was the first such degree given by an American university.

Lowell eventually obtained the deserved title 'Father of American Church and Public School Music.'

Lowell's remarkable power as a leader and organizer was due to a variety of characteristics that served him well. He had a keen intellect, patience, and the ability to learn and impart information. He was enthusiastic about everything pertaining to the application of music in public school education. Lowell published more than 50 collections of music that have sold over two million copies, and he wrote or arranged 1,697 hymn tunes. Of these 1,210 were Lowell's compositions and 487 were arrangements or adaptations from other sources.

Lowell arranged the hymn tune 'Antioch' used with "Joy to the World" in 1836 and published it in his 'Modern Psalmist' collection of 1839. Just think about it for a moment…this hymn, as we know it today, was finally completed 120 years after Isaac Watts wrote the words to this favorite Christmas hymn. Some things just take time to create and we are the blessed beneficiaries.

Lowell did cause some confusion for many years about who composed the original music for this hymn by including the phrase 'From George Frederick Handel' in his publication of the hymn. However, there has never been any proof discovered that Handel had anything to do with the music for "Joy To The World." The confusion can be attributed to the fact that Lowell may have used a couple excerpts from Handel's 'Messiah' music when Lowell made his 'original' musical arrangement for this hymn.

In the later years of Lowell's life, he bought an estate, which he named 'Silver Spring,' on the side of the Orange Mountains in Orange, New Jersey, and the days were passed there with his sons, but his devotion to musical study and composition continued to the end of his long life of 80 years, despite failing eyesight. Lowell's family gave his vast library of music books to Yale University in 1875.

FELIX MENDELSSOHN

Composer of music for "Hark! The Herald Angels Sing" in 1840

Born on February 3, 1809 in Hamburg, Germany
Died on November 4, 1847 in Leipzig, Germany

Felix Mendelssohn was the second of four children born to Abraham and Leah (Salomon) Mendelssohn. His father was a banker and Felix grew up in a privileged and influential environment. His grandfather was the famous philosopher, Moses Mendelssohn (1729-1786). Felix is considered to be the first of the great Romantic era composers, the last of the great Classical period composers, and the most successful musician of the 19th century.

Felix's family converted from Judaism to Christianity in 1816 and added 'Bartholdy' to the end of their surname, thus his full name became Jakob Ludwig Felix Mendelssohn-Bartholdy. Felix, along with his beloved sister, Fanny, learned to play the piano at a young age under the instruction of their mother and Felix made his public debut on the keyboard at the age of nine. At the age of 17 he amazed everyone in the world of music by composing the overture to "A Midsummer Night's Dream." Felix attended Berlin University from 1826-29. He studied music in Weimar and Berlin, including formal piano training under Carl Zelter. Felix loved the music of J.S Bach, Mozart and Beethoven, and he excelled as a pianist, conductor, educator, and an organizer of musical events. Felix was one of the first conductors to use a baton. In March of 1829, he conducted a full-scale performance of Bach's" "St. Matthew Passion," which led to a new appreciation of Bach's works around the world. In 1833, he became the music director in Dusseldorf, and then in 1835 he seized the opportunity to become the conductor of the famed Gewandhaus Orchestra in Leipzig.

Felix married Cecile Charlotte Sophie Jeanrenaud, the daughter of a clergyman in the French Reformed Church, on March 28, 1837 in Leipzig. They had five children born to them from 1838 to 1845. Felix's achievements included the founding of the Conservatory of Leipzig in 1842, which raised the standards for the training of musicians. Unfortunately, Felix stayed so busy that he would often border on exhaustion and at the young age of 38 he died from a series of strokes, just a few months after the death of his cherished older sister, Fanny, from a stroke in May of 1847. It is said that Felix was beloved by all who knew him. He was unselfish and pure in his private life, and unspoiled by his wealth and acclaim.

Felix composed the music used with "Hark! The Herald Angels Sing" in 1840. It came from the second movement of his 'Festgesang' (Festival Song) cantata, which was composed to commemorate the 400th anniversary of the invention of the printing press. His music was adapted to this famous Christmas hymn in 1855 by William Cummings. The music was first published with the words to "Hark! The Herald Angels Sing" in an 1857 'Congregational Hymn and Tune Book.' Felix admitted to the printers of the "Festgesang" music that he felt the original words were not too well suited to the piece and felt that it would be better suited matched with other words. Unfortunately, Felix died in 1847 and never heard his music used with the words to "Hark! The Herald Angels Sing," but I am sure he would be pleased with the marriage of these words to his music.

EMILY HUNTINGTON MILLER

Author of "Jolly Old St. Nicholas" in 1865

Born on October 22, 1833 in Brooklyn, Connecticut
Died on November 2, 1913 in Northfield, Minnesota

Emily was the daughter of a Methodist pastor, Thomas Huntington, and Pauline (Clark). She displayed literary skills while in her school days by being a prolific contributor of sketches, short stories, serials, poems and miscellaneous articles to newspapers and magazines. Over 100 of her poems were eventually set to music.

She graduated from Oberlin College in Ohio in 1857 and three years later in 1860 she married a teacher, John E. Miller. Emily served as an Assistant Editor and then Editor-in-Chief of 'The Little Corporal' children's magazine; Associate Editor of 'The Ladies Home Journal'; and co-founder of 'St. Nicholas', a publication for children. She was connected with the Chautauqua Literary and Scientific Circle from its beginning and served as president of the Chautauqua Woman's Club for four years.

Emily was prominently connected with the Woman's Foreign Missionary Society of the Methodist Church and was a Trustee of Northwestern University. In 1874 she was involved with organizing the 'National Woman's Christian Temperance Union' in Cleveland, Ohio.

Her husband John died in 1882, and in 1891 she was appointed Dean of Women at Northwestern University in Illinois. All of her lifetime achievements led to her being named one of the 'women of the 19th century" in 1893.

Emily wrote the original words to 'Jolly Old St. Nicholas' in a poem titled 'Lilly's Secret' and it was published in 'The Little Corporal Magazine' in December of 1865.

In 1874, James Ramsey Murray published Emily's original poem words with music in his 'School Chimes: A New School Music Book' under the song title of 'Jolly Old St. Nicholas.' Murray is believed to be the composer of the music for the song. Changes to some of the lyrics were made over the next few years by various editors.

The words to the song as we know them today were first published with music in John Piersol McCaskey's 'Franklin Square Song Collection, No. 1' in 1881.

Emily died at the home of her brother in Northfield, Minnesota, just two weeks after an 80th birthday celebration for her was held at her brother's home. One of her friends described her as "frail in body, but her rare gifts of mind and heart were ever cheerfully placed at the service of humanity."

It's obvious that Emily devoted herself to many 'causes' during her lifetime. Her famous Christmas song 'Jolly Old St. Nicholas' reminds me of a Statler Brothers Christmas song from 1978 with the title 'I Believe In Santa's Cause', which certainly rings true in my book!

JOSEPH MOHR

Author of "Silent Night" in 1816

Born on December 11, 1792 in Salzburg, Austria
Died on December 5, 1848 in Wagrain, Austria

Josephus Franciscus Mohr was born into poverty, the son of Franz and Anna (Schoiber) Mohr. His father was a soldier and his mother was a seamstress. Franz Mohr served in the army as one of the archbishop's musketeers and sadly left Anna and Joseph on their own to eek out a living. They lived in a small room at 31 Steingasse, in the old part of Salzburg, with an elderly grandmother of Joseph's. The cathedral choirmaster, Johann Hiernle, became a foster father to the young student, recognized his musical talent, and saw to it that Joseph received a proper education at a grammar school in Kremsmunster, Upper Austria, where he received honors for his work. Joseph completed his education at the archdiocesan seminary in Salzburg and became a Roman Catholic priest on August 21, 1815. When Joseph wrote the German words to "Stille Nacht" in 1816, he was serving as a priest in a pilgrimage church in Mariapfarr, Austria. Due to a bout with poor health, Joseph was sent back to Salzburg for hospitalization and after his recovery was assigned a

post as assistant pastor at the St. Nicholas Church in Oberndorf on August 25, 1817.

It was here that Joseph struck up a friendship with Franz Gruber, the eventual composer of "Stille Nacht." Until 1995, it had been thought that Joseph wrote his famous poem in 1818, but an original manuscript from approximately 1820 was discovered, indicating that Joseph wrote the poem in 1816, and this copy happens to be the only known existing manuscript signed by Joseph in his own handwriting. In the upper right hand corner of this manuscript, Joseph gives full credit for the composition of the music to Franz Gruber. Joseph was still a young man, in his first year of service as a priest, when he wrote "Silent Night." No one knows exactly what event inspired Joseph to write his poem, but the most plausible traditional story is that he had been called out on a snowy night to bless a newborn baby in the home of one of his peasant parishioners. The birth of the baby near Christmas time, combined with a quiet walk home through the silently falling snow caused him to return to his study and pen the poem that generations of people have enjoyed ever since. Before another Christmas could come around, Joseph was transferred from Oberndorf, the birthplace of "Silent Night," on October 19, 1819 and he went on to serve parishes at Kuchl, Golling, Vigaun, Adnet, Anthering, Eugendorf and Hof. In 1828, he was appointed pastor of the parish at Hintersse, where he served for ten years, before being transferred to the parish at Wagrain on March 4, 1837, where he served another ten years before dying from a lung disease in 1848. Unfortunately, Joseph was never officially recognized around the world as the author of the hymn until after his death. Joseph died penniless in Wagrain, reportedly because he had donated all his earnings to be used for the care of the elderly, and the education of the children in the area. One report described Joseph as "a reliable friend of mankind, and towards the poor...a gentle, helping father."

The Joseph Mohr School is now located across the street from his grave in the churchyard at Wagrain. Thank you Joseph Mohr, for writing your lovely, reverent poem, we know as the Christmas hymn "Silent Night."

JAMES MONTGOMERY

Author of "Angels From The Realms Of Glory" in 1816

Born on November 4, 1771 in Irvine,
Ayrshire, Scotland
Died on April 30, 1854 in Sheffield, York, England

James was the son of Nathaniel and Nancy (Wilson) Montgomery, Irish Moravian missionaries. When he was only six years old, James' parents left for the West Indies to serve as missionaries there, and he was left in the care of the Brethren of Fulneck who kept a boys' boarding school. It was there that James said later "whatever we did was done in the name and for the sake of Jesus Christ, whom we were taught to regard as a friend and brother." James was raised and trained a total of eight years by the Brethren for the Moravian ministry. It was during this period of time that his parents died in the mission field while in the West Indies in 1780.

James began to write poetry at the age of ten after being influenced by the Moravian hymns used by the Brethren. At fourteen he was dismissed from school because of his preoccupation with writing poetry and so he went to work as an apprentice in a bakery. When he was sixteen he ran away to London and tried unsuccessfully to sell some of his poetry, so he took a job as a clerk in a bookstore. In 1792, he answered a want ad for a job at a weekly newspaper, the 'Sheffield Register,' and it was there that he began his life's work. Two years later, the editor of the newspaper, Joseph Gales, left England for fear of prosecution in connection to some radical political articles he had published. James became the owner and editor of the paper at the age of twenty-two, changed the name to the 'Sheffield Iris,' and maintained the publication for the next thirty-one years. James became an advocate of social reform and was imprisoned twice for his outspoken articles on national issues. The outbreak of the French Revolution took place in 1789 and the British government was trying to raise an army for an expected war with France, but the town of Sheffield was more interested in fighting for the rights of man and ousting the aristocrats. James printed a song celebrating the fall of the Bastille and was jailed for it in York Castle. Shortly after his release he printed his objection to the way a military commander had put down a riot in Sheffield, and was jailed again for seditious libel. Not surprisingly, he spent his time in prison writing poetry.

James wrote the words to "Angels From the Realms of Glory" in 1816 and he published the poem under the title "Nativity" in his Sheffield Iris on December 24. It is one of nearly 400 hymns written by James, and probably his most famous. His Christmas poem became universally popular after its publication in his 'Christian Psalmist' hymnbook of 1825 under the title "Good Tidings of Great Joy to All People" and was used with the tune to "Angels We Have Heard On High." Henry Thomas Smart composed the current tune for this hymn in 1867, and it was at this time that the hymn took on the lasting title of "Angels From the Realms of Glory." James wrote other poems that became Christmas hymns, but for the most part they remained in obscurity and never began to approach the popularity of his "Angels From the Realms of Glory."

In 1825, James gave up his paper to devote himself to literary and philanthropic pursuits, such as composing poetry and lecturing about it, advocating foreign missions, humanizing the lot of boy chimneysweeps, and working for the abolition of the slave trade. Also, James worked with evangelical Anglicans to win acceptance for hymn singing in their churches. Together with his friend and fellow hymn writer, Thomas Cotterill, James won the approval of the archbishop of York for the use of a hymnal they had compiled. For a time, James left the Moravian religious fold and became tolerant of the Anglicans, Baptists, Methodists, Catholics, Unitarians and Quakers, but he returned to his Moravian roots at the age of forty-three.

A reformed British government in 1833 gave him a royal pension of 200 pounds per year. He bought a magnificent estate called 'The Mount' at the west end of the town of Sheffield and lived there in comfort until he died in his sleep on April 30, 1854.

JAMES RAMSEY MURRAY

Composer of music for "Away In A Manger" in 1887

Born on March 17, 1841 in
Andover (Ballard-Vale), Massachusetts
Died on March 10, 1905 in Cincinnati, Ohio

James was born in Massachusetts one month before John Tyler became the first U.S. Vice-President to complete the un-expired term of a president, when President Harrison died after only one month in office. James's Scottish parents, Walter and Christain, had come to America just the year before in 1840. The time period in which James spent his youth proved to be an exciting time in American history. From 1841 to 1856 events that occurred in America included the opening of the Oregon Trail, the invention of the telegraph, the Mexican War, the beginning of the California Gold Rush, the founding of the Republican Party, and the first railroad train crossed the Mississippi.

James was fortunate to receive an excellent early musical education at the Musical Institute in North Reading, Massachusetts from 1856 to 1859. Lowell Mason, George Root, and William Bradbury, the most famous musicians of the day, had founded the Musical Institute in 1853. His teachers recognized the talent in James and regarded him as one of the finest young musical minds they had ever encountered. James used his education to later become a music editor and a hymn writer of a great number of Sunday school songs, gospel songs, and religious anthems. Unfortunately, before he could finish his musical schooling and begin his professional life in music the Civil War came along, so James enlisted in the Union Army in 1862 and served in the military band. It was during the war year of 1863 that he composed his first song "Daisy Deane" while camped in Virginia. Two years later, while he was still in the Union Army in 1865, James wrote the words and music to two other war songs titled "Sleep, Sacred Dust of Noble Dead" and "This Hallowed Place We Seek." After the war James returned home to teach piano, but soon after began his career as a music editor with the Root & Cady Company in Chicago in 1865. He was employed there until the famous Chicago fire of 1871, which destroyed the Root & Cady building. James married Isabella (Taylor) in Andover, Massachusetts in 1868.

James opted to teach music in the Andover public school system for the next decade before becoming a music editor with the John Church Company from 1881 until his death in 1905. Two popular music periodicals that James edited during his time with the Root & Cady and John Church companies were 'The Song Messenger' from 1865-71 and 'The Musical Visitor' from 1881-1905.

It was during his time at the John Church Company that James composed and arranged the music for "Away In A Manger." The poem for this Christmas lullaby was first published anonymously in Philadelphia, in an 1885 children's Sunday school book titled 'Little Children's Book.' James published the verses along with his music in an 1887 collection called 'Dainty Songs for Lads and Lasses for Use in the Kindergarten, School and Home.' James titled the lullaby "Luther's Cradle Hymn" which for many years created confusion regarding the authorship of the verses. For years and decades afterwards Martin Luther was assumed to be the author, but musicologists have since proved this attribution to be incorrect. James named his tune 'Mueller' and it is this contribution to our traditional Christmas music for which James is remembered today.

JOHN MASON NEALE

Author of "Good King Wenceslas" in 1853
English translator of "O Come, O Come Emmanuel"
in 1851
English translator of "Good Christian Men, Rejoice"
in 1853

Born on January 24, 1818 in London, England
Died on August 6, 1866 in East Grimstead, England

John Mason Neale was born into an Evangelical family in Holborn, London, the only son of four children to Rev. Cornelius and Susanna Neale. Unfortunately, his father died when he was only five. His early education included private tutoring and some time spent at Shelbourne Grammar School. John then attended Trinity College in Cambridge from 1836 to 1840 where he developed an interest in church architecture. While at Cambridge he came under the influence of the Oxford Movement, and he joined some friends in forming the Cambridge Camden Society of Antiquarians, which championed the cause of "Victorian Gothic."

In 1842, John married Sarah Norman Webster, and they had four daughters by the names of Agnes, Mary, Catherine, and Margaret. Also in 1842, John

was ordained a priest, but health problems, including a chronic lung disease, brought on by excessive work, prevented his remaining in the ministry. John had to relocate for a time to the Madiera Islands off the northwest coast of Africa in order to recuperate from his illnesses. From 1846-66 he was able to serve as Warden of Sackville College, even though being a semi-invalid. The institution there served as a home for impoverished old men. His pay was a mere 27 pounds per year, but the position allowed him the time he needed to work on his studies of church history and literature.

John founded the 'Society of St. Margaret' in 1854, one of the first Anglican convent sisterhoods. His 'sisters of charity' worked with the impoverished and sick in nearby villages, with John serving as their pastor, confessor and administrator. Trinity College in Hartford, Connecticut conferred a Doctor of Divinity degree upon John in 1860.

With the exception of his original carol "Good King Wenceslas," John is most widely recognized by his translations and adaptations of ancient and medieval works in Greek and Latin, which he worked on throughout his life, earning him the title 'Prince of Translators.' His classical music training, and an ear for poetic rhythms, enabled him to retain the rhythms of the original songs, while adapting his translated texts to suitable melodies. John could read and write in 21 languages and it is estimated that he had a hand in producing over 400 hymns and carols.

John wrote "Good King Wenceslas" as a subject for a children's song, and it is based on a legend about Wenceslas, the real life Duke of Bohemia, who ruled from 922-29 A.D. Wenceslas became renowned for his kindness to his subjects, especially on Christmas Eve, Christmas Day, and St. Stephen's Day, which is on December 26. Unfortunately, his envious twin brother, Boleslav, had Wenceslas murdered.

The verses of this carol form a dialogue between the king and his page about a poor peasant and how the king took mercy on him. The carol first appeared in print in John's song collection titled "Carol's for Christmastide" in 1853.

John translated another Christmas hymn, "O Come, O Come Emmanuel" in 1851 and then revised his translation in 1853. After the music by Thomas Helmore was adapted to the translation in 1854, the hymn quickly became popular. The original Latin version of the song did not include the now popular refrain, and a musical setting that would accommodate the stanzas and the refrain "Rejoice! Rejoice! Emmanuel shall come to thee O Israel" was formed out of some Catholic liturgical chants.

The hymn has now been translated into over 125 languages. John also provided us with the English translation of "Good Christian Men, Rejoice," which he included in his carol collection "Carols for Christmastide" in 1853.

John's health finally broke for good in early 1866 and after five months of acute suffering he died on the 'Feast of the Transfiguration' on August 6, 1866.

FREDERICK OAKELEY

English Translator of "Adeste Fideles" in 1852

Born on September 5, 1802 in Shrewsbury, England
Died on January 29, 1880 in Islington,
London, England

Frederick Oakeley was the youngest son of eleven children born to Sir Charles and Helena (Beatson) Oakeley. His grandfather, William, was a minister, and his father was a one-time governor of Madras around 1792. Frederick was shortsighted, small in stature and lame, but he made up for his shortcomings through his writings and charm of conversation. As with other Englishmen featured in this book, we know little about the formative years of Frederick before the start of his formal higher education. However, we do know of other European historical events that occurred during his first twenty years. The continent saw the rise and fall of Napoleon from 1803 to 1815. The British were engaged in war with the United States from 1812 to 1814. The future Queen Victoria was born in 1819 and Napoleon died the year that Frederick entered Oxford. Frederick was educated at Christ Church, in Oxford, where he received his Bachelor of Arts degree in 1824. In 1827, he was elected a Fellow of Balliol, and in 1828 he took his holy orders. Frederick was first a clergyman in the Church of England and later in the Roman Catholic Church. In 1832, he became a clergyman at Lichfield Cathedral, moved on to Whitehall in 1837 (the same year that Queen Victoria of England began her 63 year reign), and then to Margaret Street Chapel (the predecessor to the well-known All Saints Margaret Street Church) in London in 1839.

Frederick was one of the Tractarian authors during the Oxford Movement in England, which advocated that certain Roman Catholic practices be restored in the Church of England. The Movement began in 1833 and gained favor for about ten years before it began to disintegrate with the secession of many of its members to the Roman Catholic Church. Frederick's involvement with the movement created great controversy, leading to his suspension and eventual resignation from the Church of England in 1845. He later joined the Roman Catholic Church, where he was ordained in 1847, and then became Canon of Westminster diocese from 1852-80. For many years he was known to work among the poor of Westminster, and he had multiple literary works of his published from 1837 to 1871. Others remember Frederick as being a kind, good, lovable and scholarly man and "an elegant writer and great lover of music." The general consensus of his piers was that he was "not as good at preaching as he was being a musician."

Frederick's fame rests primarily with his translation of the popular 18th century hymn "Adeste Fidelis" into English in 1841. Initially, the translation was simply for use at his Margaret Street Chapel. In 1852, after Frederick had converted to Roman Catholicism, he changed his 1841 English title of the song from "Ye Faithful Approach Ye" to "O Come All Ye Faithful." The completed hymn with its fresh new title first appeared in Rev. F.H. Murray's 1852 collection titled 'A Hymnal For Use In The English Church' published in London. Frederick believed that if congregations had good literary texts to sing...they would sing well. I guess it's safe to say that "Adeste Fidelis" proved his point.

JAMES PIERPONT

Author & Composer of "Jingle Bells" in 1850

Born on April 25, 1822 in Medford, Massachusetts
Died on January 1, 1893 in Winter Haven, Florida

James Lord Pierpont was one of six children born to the Rev. John and Mary (Sheldon Lord) Pierpont. James displayed an interest in music at an early age by learning to play the organ as a child in his father's Hollis Street Unitarian Church, as well as singing in the church choir. As a boy, and seemingly throughout his life, James never managed to be fully content with his place in the world and is perhaps best described as a 19th century 'rolling stone.' In 1832, the ten-year old James was sent off to school in New Hampshire. In a letter to his mother, James wrote about taking a sleigh ride through the New England snow (an event that no doubt influenced the young boy enough to later write his song about sleighing when he was pushing 30 years of age.) When he was fourteen he ran away from home and worked on a commercial whaling vessel (the Shark) for about ten years. When James returned to Medford, he married Mellicent Cowee (1824-1856) on September 4, 1846, and the couple had three children together, John, Mary, and Josiah. When the California gold rush began in

1849, James left his family back in Massachusetts and traveled to San Francisco, where he opened a business, which unfortunately burned to the ground shortly thereafter. He then returned to Medford, but he did leave a trace of his short stay in California in the fact that his name is found on the rolls of the Unitarian Church in San Francisco, where he served on the music committee for that church.

It was during his days in California that he reminisced with others about the sleigh rides he had often watched take place back in New England in previous winters, and he began formulating and writing the song "Jingle Bells" in 1850. Once he was back in New England in 1851, James attempted to put the finishing touches on his sleighing song. He then visited Mrs. Otis Waterman (Mary Gleason Waterman) who possessed the only piano in Medford, Massachusetts. The piano was actually owned by William Webber, who ran the West Medford singing school and boarded with Mrs. Waterman. James played his song for Mrs. Waterman in order to obtain her opinion of it. Her reply was that it was a "merry little jingle" and he should have a lot of success with it. Mary Waterman recorded in her diary that she allegedly helped James to write the chorus for "Jingle Bells." James had carried the song around in his head for a long time before it was finally published for sale in September of 1857 when Oliver Ditson and Company of Boston published it under the title "One Horse Open Sleigh." Copies of the music sold for 25 cents each. James first performed his newly published song for a Thanksgiving program at a large Boston church where he taught Sunday school. Two years later it was reprinted with the now famous title "Jingle Bells" and the song's popularity increased. The original chorus music has been changed over time, but the words and the music for the verses are the same as Pierpont composed them. "Jingle Bells" was not the first song that James had written or had copyrighted, for there is a record of at least thirteen others between the years 1852-56, however, none of these ever brought him fame or fortune, and neither did "Jingle Bells" in his lifetime. Unfortunately, Mellicent Pierpont never saw her husband's song published, because she died from tuberculosis in 1856.

James relocated to Savannah, Georgia by 1857 to

join his older brother, John Pierpont Jr., who was the minister for a Unitarian congregation in that city. James took a post as the organist and music director of the church. On September 24, 1857, he married Eliza Jane Purse, nine years younger than James, and the daughter of a Savannah, Georgia mayor. They went on to have four children together. Lillie, the only daughter and eldest child, became a music teacher, and the three boys were named Thomas, Juriah, and Maynard. James's children from his first marriage remained in Massachusetts and were raised by grandparents.

The 1860 census lists James as being a 'clerk and collector.' James soon joined the Isle of Hope Volunteers to the Confederacy, and by 1862 was serving in Company H of the 5th Georgia Volunteer Cavalry as a company clerk. During the war, he wrote patriotic Confederate songs including "Our Battle Flag," "Strike for the South" and "We Conquer or Die." His father, John, enlisted in the Union Army at an advanced age and served as a chaplain, so it turned out that father and son were on opposing sides during the Civil War. After the war, James seems to have stopped writing songs and went into the hardware business, but soon failed in that venture. In 1869, James moved to Florida, and in the 1870 census, he was listed as a 'professor of music' at Quitman Academy, in Quitman, Florida.

In 1880, James's son, Juriah, who became a successful medical doctor, renewed the copyright on "Jingle Bells," but the family never made much money from it, as the song did not really catch on until the 20th century. James was working as a deputy postmaster by 1880, and died thirteen years later at his son's home in Winter Haven, Florida, a relatively poor man, but with his name still attached to the most famous secular Christmas song of all-time. Actually, if you read the lyrics, you will find that it is not specifically a Christmas song, but we just naturally tend to associate sleigh riding with the Christmas season, so that is when the song is primarily played and sung.

Per his request, James was buried in Laurel Grove cemetery beside his brother-in-law, Thomas Purse, who was killed in the first Battle of Bull Run during the Civil War. Although James died poor, his nephew, John Pierpont (J.P.) Morgan, only fifteen years younger then James, went on to achieve huge financial success as the most famous banker and financier of the 19th century. Morgan once referred to his uncle as a "good-for-nothing." Well, J.P., if you were alive today, I'm sure you would be surprised by the enduring popularity of "Jingle Bells," and to find that the name of your Uncle James has found eternal fame as the creator of the world famous, and most frequently performed Christmas song of all-time.

LEWIS HENRY REDNER

Composer of music for "O Little Town of Bethlehem" in 1868

Born on December 15, 1830 in
Philadelphia, Pennsylvania
Died on August 29, 1908 in
Atlantic City, New Jersey

Lewis Redner, of Dutch ancestry, was one of five children born to Lewis and Catherine (Snyder) Redner and raised in Philadelphia. At the time of his birth, Philadelphia was the largest city in the United States. The historical record is silent on the first sixteen years of Lewis's life. There is no information available on his early musical education and so one can only speculate that he learned to play the organ from his parents, or perhaps was a self-taught musician, as was often the case in those days. We do know that when he was only sixteen, Lewis entered the working world and went into real estate, making it his lifetime occupation, and over time he became a very wealthy real estate broker in his hometown.

Lewis served as the organist at four different churches before becoming the organist at Holy Trinity Church in Philadelphia where Phillips Brooks was the pastor.

Lewis was also a devoted churchman and served as the Sunday school superintendent at Holy Trinity for 19 years. During those years, Lewis, a bachelor, raised the attendance of children at the church from three-dozen to over one thousand. He was also instrumental in starting an endowment fund, which still supports the work of Holy Trinity Church today.

Lewis composed the music to "O Little Town of Bethlehem" in 1868. He had resigned as organist at Holy Trinity Church in 1864, but continued to serve in other areas of the church, and he was working with the Sunday school when he was asked by Brooks to write the tune for this hymn. As with the famous Christmas hymn "Silent Night," the music for this hymn was composed within 24 hours of when it was first sang at a church program. Lewis had struggled with composing an appropriate tune for this hymn for at least a week before it was to be performed. Finally, at about midnight on Saturday night a melody came to him. The words and tune were hastily printed on leaflets and sung on Christmas morning by six Sunday school teachers and thirty-six children. Redner always insisted that the melody, which came to him in the middle of the night before the program, was "a gift from heaven."

Reverend William R. Huntington is credited with designating the name of the tune for this hymn as "St. Louis" in honor of 'Lewis' Redner. Huntington first published this hymn in his "The Church Porch" collection of songs in 1874, but the lasting popularity of the hymn was advanced by its inclusion in the Episcopal Church hymnal of 1892. Lewis and Phillips Brooks teamed up on another little known Christmas song titled "Everywhere, Everywhere, Christmas Tonight."

Lewis had gone to Atlantic City in 1908 to recuperate from an illness, but died there on August 29.

Neither Lewis nor Phillips ever expected their hymn to live on beyond that first performance in 1868. Thankfully for all of us, after six years of strictly local use, the song found its way into a song collection and then eventually into an untold number of hymnals, so that the world could continue to sing it forever more...every Christmas.

CHRISTINA GEORGINA ROSSETTI

Author of "In The Bleak Midwinter" in 1872
Author of "Love Came Down At Christmas" in 1885

Born on December 5, 1830 in London, England
Died on December 29, 1894 in London, England

Christina Rossetti was the youngest of four children born to Italian parents, Gabriele and Frances (Polidori) Rossetti. In her early years she spent much of her time with her grandfather in the country, allowing her to be exposed to nature...the subject of many of her poems. She enjoyed the country, because most of her life she lived in the city of London. She was a healthy young child, but was often ill during her adolescence.

Her family had strong ties to the Church of England and Christina's sister, Maria, joined an Anglican sisterhood. Christina never married and lived with her parents. In 1848 she became engaged to James Collinson, but the engagement ended after he converted to Roman Catholicism in 1850. Christina briefly pursued the possibility of teaching or nursing, but eventually turned to writing. She went on to become one of the most important women poets of 19th century England, sometimes using the pseudonym, Ellen Alleyne. Her family encouraged her to write, and through her brothers, William and Dante, she was introduced to many of the leading people and ideas of the day. Dante succeeded in convincing 'Macmillian's Magazine' to publish three of her early poems. Christina returned the favor by often modeling for Dante's drawings and paintings.

Her father's eyesight and health failed in 1853, so she and her mother tried operating a day school in an attempt to support the family, but the venture only lasted one year. Christina concentrated on her poetry, while suffering from a recurring illness, which was sometimes diagnosed as angina, and other times as tuberculosis. In 1862, her first, and perhaps most beloved collection of poetry was published. During the 1860's she fell in love with Charles Cayley, but refused to marry him in 1866 because she found he was not a Christian. In the 1870's, Christina continued to write her poetry and work for the Society for Promoting Christian Knowledge, even though in 1871 she was troubled physically by contracting Grave's disease, and emotionally by Dante's nervous breakdown in 1872. The appearance of the once beautiful young lady was transformed by the life threatening Grave's disease. Her brother William wrote that "her hair fell out, her skin became discolored, and her eyes bulged."

It was in 1872 that Christina wrote the words to her Christmas poem "In the Bleak Midwinter." 'Scribner's Magazine' had requested a seasonal poem from her to publish in their January 1872 magazine issue. The text was published again in her own poetry collection of 1875. In 1885 she penned the Christmas poem "Love Came Down At Christmas." It was first published that year in her collection of poetry titled "Time Flies; a Reading Diary." These two poems, which were later turned into Christmas hymns, qualify Christina as one of the first women in history to have her name attached to famous Christmas music.

Christina died silently in bed on December 29, 1894, after a two-year battle with cancer, surrounded by pictures of her loved ones, favorite novels and paintings, and a stack of her manuscript verses.

EDMUND HAMILTON SEARS

Author of "It Came Upon the Midnight Clear"
in 1849
Author of "Calm, On the Listening Ear of Night"
in 1834

Born on April 6, 1810 in Sandisfield, Massachusetts
Died on January 14, 1876 in Weston, Massachusetts

Edmund Hamilton Sears was the youngest of three sons born to Joseph and Lucy (Smith) Sears. The Sears family was descended from Richard Sears who came from Holland to the Plymouth Colony of America in 1620. Edmund grew up on a farm within sight of the Berkshire Hills, in Sandisfield, Massachusetts. The Hills are a range of mountains in Berkshire County, located in western Massachusetts, which stretches out along the Hoosic River, and the town of Sandisfield is located on the lower edge of the Hills. Edmund told his friend and colleague, Chandler Robbins, that as a child he had fancied the hilltops to rise up near heaven, where "bright-robed messengers alighted and rested, as they came and went on their errands of love."

Though both of his parents encouraged his love of study as a young student, the chores of farm labor prevented his regular school attendance. From his father, Edmund learned to appreciate poetry, and as a boy on the farm "when I was at work, some poem was always singing through my brain." From both parents he learned the importance of moral duty, and this led to his eventual service in the ministry. In 1831, his education was advanced enough for his admission as a sophomore at Union College in Schenectady, New York, from where he graduated in 1834. It was while at Union that he won a college prize for his poetry. Upon graduation Edmund studied law for nine months in Sandisfield and then did some teaching at Brattleboro (Vermont) Academy, before studying for the ministry under Addison Brown, minister of the Unitarian Church in Brattleboro. Influenced by the writings of Boston ministers William Ellery Channing and Henry Ware, Edmund went on to study at the Harvard Theological School in Cambridge, Massachusetts from 1834 to 1837. In his first year at this school Sears wrote his first Christmas carol "Calm on the Listening Ear of Night." While doing student preaching in Barnstable, Massachusetts, Edmund met his future wife, Ellen Bacon, and they were married on November 7, 1839. The couple went on to have four children, named Katharine, Francis, Edmund and Horace.

The American Unitarian Association supported Edmunds' work as a missionary in the frontier area around Toledo, Ohio. In late 1838, he filled in at the vacated pulpit for the First Congregational Church and Society in Wayland, in eastern Massachusetts. The church was impressed with his character and his preaching ability and asked him to stay on at their parish. He accepted the position and the church ordained and installed him as their minister in February of 1839. Though he found Wayland pleasing, Edmund soon learned that to provide for his family he needed to serve a larger, more prosperous church. He accepted and established a successful ministry at the Congregational Church in Lancaster from 1840 to 1847. However, his ministry there was cut short by illness and depression. After his illness he was unable to preach in a voice loud enough to be heard by a large congregation or to sustain the work of a large parish. He returned to Wayland for a year of rest and recovery, and when his health improved, he was recalled to the smaller Wayland parish and served there from 1848 to 1865.

It was during this time under a lighter workload that he spent much of his spare time writing. Years later Edmund explained that he had never been ambitious for a large city pulpit, or attracted to the prominence of such a position. Rather, he was drawn to and enjoyed "the quiet beauty of Wayland with its simple way of life and little parish."

Edmund began to write the words to "It Came Upon the Midnight Clear" in 1846 towards the end of his ministry in Lancaster and during his struggle with illness and personal melancholy. By the time he finished the poem and had it published in 1849 other events around the world had influenced the wording in his hymn, including the news of revolution in Europe, the United States' war with Mexico, the California gold rush, tensions between the northern and southern states in the U.S., and a severe cholera epidemic along the Oregon Trail. In his now famous Christmas hymn, Edmund wrote about the world being dark and full of "sin and strife," and not hearing the Christmas message. It was not until he had changed pulpits and his health had recovered that his famous Christmas poem was first published in the December 29, 1849 issue of the Unitarian periodical "The Christian Register" in Boston, under the title "Peace On Earth." Even though his Christmas hymn has been criticized for not mentioning the Christ-child, Edmund personally believed in a Christ fully human and fully divine, the incarnation of the Divine Word, and the mediator who alone can bridge "the awful gulf between God and man." Edmunds' Unitarian beliefs were considered conservative in his day and he wrote a number of theological works influential among liberal Protestants, inside and outside the Unitarian fold. He was more of a Unitarian in name rather than by conviction and once stated "although I was educated in the Unitarian denomination, I believe and preach the Divinity of Christ." (William Channing founded the Unitarian denomination in 1819. The Unitarian church denies the holiness of the Trinity and believes in only one Divine Being.)

The hymn "It Came Upon the Midnight Clear" became the first American Christmas song with international appeal, and was the first Christmas song written by an American to achieve lasting popularity.

It was after Richard Storrs Willis' music was attached to Edmund's poem in 1850 that the song gained popularity, but the public praise Edmund received dismayed him somewhat, because he was one, as already mentioned, who preferred to lead a quiet, serene life. It was after the Civil War that Edmund resigned his Wayland pastorate in order to spend most his time writing, but he returned to the ministry in 1866 when he accepted a position with the First Parish Church in Weston, Massachusetts, just seven miles down the road from Wayland. The original manuscript of "It Came Upon the Midnight Clear" is preserved in the Sears Memorial Chapel at the Weston church. Other papers relating to the life and ministry of Edmund Sears are kept at the Wayland Historical Society and at the Andover-Harvard Theological Library in Cambridge, Massachusetts. Edmund is credited with writing between 40 and 50 hymns, however, only the two mentioned in this book relate to the subject of Christmas.

Edmund also served as the associate editor of the 'Monthly Religious Magazine' from 1859 to 71. In the summer of 1873 Edmund enjoyed a tour of Europe, but in 1874, while working in his garden, he took a nasty fall from a tree and from that time on he was rarely free of illness and pain until his death in 1876. Edmund is remembered as a humble, pious man who overcame poor health to write one of our favorite Christmas hymns "It Came Upon the Midnight Clear." Thank you ever so much, Mr. Sears.

HENRY THOMAS SMART

Composer of music for "Angels From The Realms of Glory" in 1867

Born on October 26, 1813 in London, England
Died on July 6, 1879 in London, England

Henry Thomas Smart was the son of a violinist and orchestra leader, Henry Smart, and Ann (Stanton Bagnold) and a nephew of Sir George Smart, who was considered one of the greatest ever English conductors. Henry studied music under his father and also with W.H. Kearns, while attending the educational institution of Highgate. As a boy, he spent free time at the Robson organ factory, where he began acquiring his profound knowledge of organ mechanics and construction, while at the same time, attending scientific lectures at the Royal Institution. As a twelve year-old, Henry displayed a talent for mechanical drawing, but he never pursued that natural ability as a career. He also declined the offer for a commission in the Indian Army, before making a four-year try at the law profession, but he gave that up for his eventual career in music.

In 1831 he became organist at the Blackburn Parish Church, where he wrote his first important work, a Reformation anthem. Henry went on to serve consecutive terms as organist at St. Philip's, Regent Street, London in 1836, at St. Giles's, Cripplegate for a short while, at St. Luke's, Old Street for 21 years beginning in 1844, and finally at St. Pancras beginning in 1865, where he served until his death. His wife's name was Julia (Rackham). They were married in 1840 and she outlived him by three years.

Henry took extra pleasure in serving as an accompanist in church services. He was one of only five organists asked to perform at the Great Exhibition of 1851, and he went on to be recognized as one of England's finest organists and composers for the organ. He favored congregational singing, and the slow, dignified style of the old psalm tunes, rather than the quicker measures, which his contemporaries were beginning to use.

All his life Henry suffered from a 'weakness in the eyes'; a terminology used for poor vision, and it was in 1864 that his eyesight began to fail rapidly. By the time he composed the music for "Angels From The Realms of Glory" in 1867 he was totally blind. Because of his blindness, Henry dictated his tune to his daughter who put the notes down on paper for him. Henry titled the music for this hymn 'Regent Square', dedicated to the Regent Square Presbyterian Church in London. The tune was first printed in the 1867 Presbyterian hymnal 'Psalms and Hymns for Divine Worship.'

Henry is known chiefly for his organ compositions, but he also wrote vocal works and part songs. By the time he was 50 years of age he had composed some 250 secular songs and edited two church hymnbooks, the 'Chorale Book' in 1856, and the Presbyterian Hymnal in 1875. He also learned organ-building skills from his father. He designed the organs in City and St. Andrew's Halls, in Glasgow, and the Town Hall, in Leeds. In 1878, a year before he died, he was sent to examine the organ at Christ Church in Dublin, Ireland. Despite the disability of blindness the last 15 years of his life, Henry continued as a composer and organist at St. Pancras Church, and wrote some of his largest works after he became blind. Henry died from liver cancer the same year that Thomas Edison perfected his invention of the light bulb, but Henry didn't need a light bulb to brighten our world through his musical contributions such as "Angels From The Realms of Glory."

JOHN STAINER

Arranger of "God Rest Ye Merry Gentlemen" in 1871
Arranger of "Here We Come A Caroling" in 1871
Arranger of "The First Noel" in 1871
Arranger of "What Child Is This?" in 1871

Born on June 6, 1840 in London, England
Died on March 31, 1901 in Verona, Italy

John Stainer was the second son of William Stainer, a schoolmaster at the parish school of St. Thomas in Southwark. William taught John to play the organ and to read music. Thankfully for us, this was just the beginning of a life dedicated to the world of music. All of his musical experiences allowed John to become one of the most important people in the advancement of Christmas music.

John joined the boy's choir of St. Paul's Cathedral in 1847 and remained in the choir until 1856. By his last year at St. Paul's he had already held organist posts at St. Benet's and St. Paul's on Upper Thames Street. Then in 1856, John was given the appointment of organist at St. Michael's College in Tenbury. Four years later he took a similar position at Magdalen College in Oxford, and a year later, he became the organist at Oxford University. John graduated from Oxford with a B.A. in 1863 and a Masters degree in 1866.

John's professional music career continued in 1872 with an appointment as organist at St. Paul's, and from 1876-89 he served as a professor of organ in the National Training School of Music. John became the principal at this school from 1882-89. Due to failing eyesight, John retired from the position of organist at St. Paul's in 1888, and for his contribution to English music was knighted by Queen Victoria as Sir John Stainer that same year. From 1889-99 John held the post as professor of music at Oxford University. Also, during his long career in music, John at various times served as president of the Plainsong and Medieval Music Society, the London Gregorian Association, and the Musical Association. He was undoubtedly a man of great influence in the musical profession. John was considered to be one of the ablest choir trainers of his generation and did valuable work in the field of musicology. I would say this is a remarkable list of lifetime accomplishments for a man who was blinded in his left eye by an accident as a boy when he was five years old. John set an inspirational example to follow for others with handicaps.

In 1871, John published a collection of Christmas songs titled "Christmas Carols New & Old." This was the first major English language carol collection, and did much to promote carols of all types. It contained 13 traditional carols and 24 new hymns. He arranged so many songs for this publication that he was often credited as being the creator, rather than arranger of the songs. His popular arrangements from this collection still sung today include "Here We Come A Caroling," "God Rest Ye Merry Gentlemen," "The First Noel" and "What Child Is This?"

John was described as a man of sincerity and integrity, and he and his wife, Eliza Cecil (Randall), gave generously, in monetary terms, to the church and other charities. John died suddenly while on a holiday trip to Verona, Italy in March of 1901.

NAHUM TATE

Author of "While Shepherds Watched Their Flocks By Night" in 1696

Born 1652 in Dublin, Ireland
Died on August 12, 1715 in Southwark,
London, England

Nahum Tate was the son of an Irish clergyman and poet, Faithful Teate, and Katherine (Kenetie) Teate. He graduated with a B.A. from Trinity College in Dublin in 1672. Nahum changed the spelling of his surname from Teate to Tate in 1677 when he began writing poetry. In 1678, Nahum relocated to London, England, where he did some writing for stage productions, primarily adapting the works of others. His greatest success in the theatre was his 1681 version of 'King Lear,' which remained popular well into the early 19th century.

Once in London, Nahum formed a friendship with the famous English poet, John Dryden, and it was probably through Dryden's influence that Nahum was appointed the third official 'Poet Laureate' of England by King William III in 1692. He served under the reigns of William & Mary, Anne, and George I. His responsibility in that post, as part of the royal household, was to compose poems for court and national occasions. The position of Poet Laureate paid Nahum 100 pounds per year. The name 'Laureate' means 'crowned with laurel' and comes from an ancient Roman tradition of honoring a person, especially poets, who had shown excellence of achievement.

Nahum authored "While Shepherds Watched Their Flocks" in 1696, four years after becoming Poet Laureate. His original poem was known as 'Song of the Angels' and was a metrical version of Luke 2:8-14 from the Bible. It was first published in 1700 in a supplement to the 1696 work by Nahum and Nicholas Brady (1659-1726) titled "New Version of the Psalms of David." His Christmas hymn was originally sang in 1703 to a tune by Thomas Este, known as "Winchester Old" in England. The tune by Este was first published in his "Whole Book of Psalms" in 1592. It was not until 1861 that Richard Storrs Willis adapted some opera music by George F. Handel to Nahum's words and created this hymn, as we know it today.

Nahum was appointed as the royal historiographer in 1702, a position that paid 200 pounds per year in addition to the pay from his other lifetime position with the royal family. In 1708, Nahum's famous hymn poem was the only Christmas song sanctioned by the Church of England for use in their worship services. This was indeed an honor of great achievement for Nahum, because at that time of the 'psalm-singing' Church of England, it was virtually impossible for a 'human composition' to be introduced into the services.

Nahum was described as an honest and quiet man, but given somewhat to "fuddling" (intoxication.) Unfortunately, Nahum not only had a drinking problem, but he failed to plan for his future, and these two problems came back to haunt him in his latter days. Despite all of his musical and literary efforts and achievements, Nahum failed to achieve financial success and died in a debtors' refuge called the 'Mint,' where he had gone in order to escape his creditors. Although Nahum's life took a tragic turn at the end... we need to be grateful for his 'pioneering' contribution to Christmas music. The 1708 achievement of having his hymn accepted by the Church of England was a pivotal point in the history of Christmas hymns.

Love and Joy Come to You

JOHN FRANCIS WADE

Author & Composer of "Adeste Fidelis" in 1751

Born 1711 in Leeds, England
Died on August 16, 1786 in Douay, France

John Francis Wade was born in the city of Leeds, in northern England, in 1711. Although we don't know all that much about Wade's personal life, we do know about the world and circumstances in which he lived as an exile in Douai, France. We can fairly confidently surmise that John came from a wealthy family of privilege in England, since he was well educated and skilled in the art of music. A few years prior to John's birth, James II was the monarch of both England and Scotland, however he made himself unpopular by supporting Catholicism in England. In 1688, the English parliament invited James's son-in-law, William of Orange, to become King of England, and he accepted the offer. James did not attempt to fight for his crown and fled the country. In 1689, the term 'Jacobite' became the name for those who supported James after his deposition. There were Jacobite rebellions in 1689 and 1708, but it was probably sometime after the rebellions of 1715 and 1719, after John had grown into adulthood, that he became a Catholic and a supporter of the cause to return a 'Stuart' monarch to the throne. He then exiled

himself to Douai by the 1740's. It was during John's days in Douai, and the time period he wrote "Adeste Fidelis," that the most famous Jacobite rebellion took place in 1745. After things went well for the Jacobite cause in that year, Charles Edward Stuart, led his Jacobite army to ultimate disaster at the 'Battle of Culloden' in 1746, which ended for good the Jacobites hopes of returning a 'Stuart' monarch to the throne.

By the 1740's, a Roman Catholic center had been established in Douai by King Philip II of Spain, with an English university that served as a haven for English religious and political refugees like John. Today, Douai is a town of about 45,000 people located in the French Flanders, on the Scarpe River, in northern France. It is a major industrial and commercial center of the coal region. The chief manufactures are foundry products, automobile parts, glass, chemicals, and printing. Douai was founded as a Roman fortress in the 4th century. The town received a charter in 1228, passed into the possession of the dukes of Burgundy in 1384, and then to the Spanish Hapsburgs in 1477. Louis XIV seized Douai in 1667, and after the War of the Spanish Succession Douai was permanently restored to France by the Peace of Utrecht in 1713.

John was a trained musician and skilled calligrapher, who made his living copying and selling music to Roman Catholic chapels, and giving music lessons to wealthy families in the community. It was the custom of these families to encourage priests with musical ability to copy music and carry it to other chapels for use in various services. His surviving beautiful manuscripts are an example of his artistic abilities and his calligraphy was much in demand because suitable printing type was not yet available in Douai. John earned the title 'Father of English Plainsong' after publishing a work entitled 'An Essay in Plainchant' in 1782.

The origins of both the text and tune to "Adeste Fidelis" were shrouded in mystery through the years until 1947 when some original manuscripts of the song were discovered. At least five original manuscripts of "Adeste Fidelis" are known to exist, with four of them in England, and all signed by Joannes Franciscus Wade. Their authenticity is verified by the paper watermarks they are printed on which dates them from the 1740's. John began writing the Latin stanzas in 1743, and then combined the text with some simple music and published the hymn in 1751, in his collection of songs known as "Cantus Diversi." His original manuscripts of this collection are preserved in the library of Stonyhurst College in Lancashire, England. His famous Christmas hymn proceeded to gain popularity with the Catholics in France, where it was used at the annual 'Benediction of the Christmas Mass.' Wade wrote four original stanzas, with three more added in the early 19th century by Jean Francois Borderies of France. Samuel Webbe published the hymn in 1782 in 'An Essay on the Church Plain Chant.' In this publication the tune as we know it today, was matched by Webbe with the

text. The first publication of the hymn in the United States was on December 29, 1800 in Benjamin Carr's "Musical Journal."

For about two hundred years the words to this hymn were alternately and inaccurately attributed to the Portuguese, Saint Bonaventura of Italy, the Germans and Cistercian monks. The music was often credited to an English organist, John Reading, but this too has been disproved with the manuscript finds in 1947.

It's nice for us that the historical record regarding this hymn has finally been set straight concerning the creation of this beautiful Christmas hymn by John Francis Wade.

ISAAC WATTS

Author of "Joy To The World" in 1719

Born on July 17, 1674 in Southampton, England
Died on November 25, 1748 in Abney Park, England

Isaac Watts was the son of a Nonconformist deacon in a dissenting Congregational church and was the oldest of nine children. At the time of Isaac's birth, his father, also named Isaac and a cobbler and tailor by trade, was in prison for his non-conformists beliefs. His mother, Sarah (Taunton) Watts, used to carry Isaac in her arms and nurse him while she stood at the prison gate to sing hymns to cheer her husband. At an early age Isaac learned to play the piano. As a boy he displayed literary genius and an aptitude for study. At the age of five, he was learning to speak Latin; at nine, Greek; at eleven, French; and at thirteen, Hebrew. When he was nine, he was stricken with smallpox, and then again in 1689, Isaac said he "had a great and dangerous illness."

While Isaac was still in his teens, he became very dissatisfied with the boring Psalm singing in their Southampton Above Bar Congregational Church. One Sunday when the eighteen year old Isaac was again being critical of Psalm singing, his father challenged him by saying "Well then, young man, why don't you give us something better to sing?" Isaac accepted the challenge and the very next Sunday produced his first hymn, to which the congregational response was enthusiastic. For the next two years, he wrote a new hymn text for the congregation every Sunday. In all, Isaac wrote approximately 600 hymns, with the bulk of them written from 1694 to 1696. He ranks as one of the most prolific male hymn writers of all-time, perhaps second only to Charles Wesley.

Isaac was very small in stature, standing a frail five feet tall. He was described as being rather homely with a big head and a long-hooked nose, but of gentle disposition. Once a young admiring woman, Elizabeth Singer, proposed marriage to Isaac by mail, and he accepted, but when the girl arrived she was disillusioned with Isaac's physical characteristics. Elizabeth declined to marry Isaac, but stayed a friend of his for more than thirty years. Unfortunately, as a result of this disappointing marital rejection, Isaac never considered marriage again or even took an interest in the opposite sex, but he did seem to enjoy children and wrote one book of songs especially for young people.

For six years between 1696 and 1701 Isaac worked as a tutor for the son of Sir John Hartopp. He preached his first sermon at age twenty-four, preaching frequently in the next three years. Isaac was ordained in 1702 and then became the pastor at the Independent Church in Mark Lane, London, at the age of twenty-seven. Unfortunately, his days as a preacher were short lived due to a severe fever, which led to a protracted illness that left him a semi-invalid. Sir Thomas Abney, one of his wealthy parishioners, invited Watts into his palatial home in 1712 and it was there that he remained a welcome guest until his death 36 years later. Isaac said that he had only intended to spend a week at the Abney home, but he quite probably set a record as the world's longest houseguest.

Today, Isaac is considered to be the 'Father of Modern English Hymnody,' because he was the first Englishman to succeed in overcoming the prejudices that opposed the introduction of hymns into English public worship. Isaac once defended the introduction of new hymns into the church by stating "we preach the gospel and pray in Christ's name, and then check the aroused devotions of Christians by giving out a song of the old dispensation." Also, Isaac wrote, "The singing of God's praise is the part of worship most closely related to heaven, but its performance among us is the worst on earth."

Isaac wrote the poem "Joy To The World" in 1719 and included it in his hymnal publication 'Psalms of David Imitated in the Language of the New Testament.' He used a translation of the last five verses of Psalm 98 from the Bible as a scripture reference for his poem. Isaac's original title for the poem was 'The Messiah's Coming and Kingdom.'

He did not purposely intend to provide the verses for one of our favorite Christmas hymns, but thankfully for us, that's the way it turned out. Dr. Edward Hodges wrote the first psalm-tune for Isaac's hymn, but that was later replaced by Lowell Mason's adapted tune 'Antioch' in 1839.

Isaac suffered a paralytic stroke in 1739, which left him permanently disabled the last nine years of his life. He was buried in the Puritan cemetery in Bunhill Fields, and a memorial monument was erected to him in Westminster Abbey.

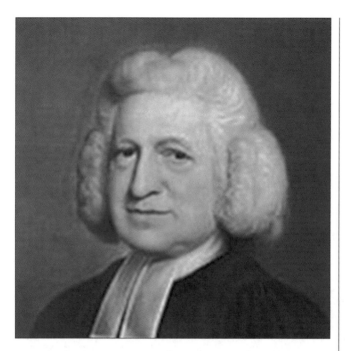

CHARLES WESLEY

Author of "Hark! The Herald Angels Sing" in 1739

Born on December 18, 1707 in Epworth, Lincolnshire, England
Died on March 29, 1788 in London, England

Charles Wesley was the eighteenth child of Samuel and Susannah (Annesley) Wesley. Samuel was an Anglican rector in Epworth, where his large family lived in an impoverished state. Then in 1709, the Wesley's humble home was destroyed by fire. Charles narrowly escaped the flames thanks to his nurse who rescued him. We owe that nurse a debt of gratitude for saving Charles' life, so that generations of people to come could enjoy his music.

Despite their troubles, his family enjoyed music and this no doubt influenced the young future hymn-writer. Charles proved to be a 'tough kid' and got into his share of fights growing up, many times in the defense of other children. He entered Westminster School in 1716 where he became a 'King's Scholar' and by 1725 was 'captain' of the school. At one point, in 1721, a wealthy Irishman offered to adopt Charles and make him his legal heir, but 13 year-old Charles refused the offer and chose to continue his way through school under very trying circumstances.

Charles entered Oxford in 1726 and while he and his brother, John, attended the university they became dissatisfied with the spiritual conditions among the students. The brothers formed an organization devoted to religious exercises. Because of their strict rules and precise methods of study, they were nicknamed 'the Methodists,' the very name that later became attached to their reform movement. Charles graduated from Oxford in 1729 and was ordained a priest in the Church of England in 1735, the same year that he went with his brother to Georgia in America, as a secretary to Governor Oglethorpe. While in America his health failed and he was forced to return to England the very next year. On his return trip, a group of German Moravians impressed and influenced Charles with their hymn singing. Charles was still recovering from his illness in England when he experienced his evangelical conversion on May 21, 1738.

John Wesley returned to England that same year of 1738 and from 1739-56 Charles was on the move with his brother preaching and organizing Methodist Societies. In spite of his hectic schedule he still found time to write hymns by the hundreds. He composed songs on horseback, in stagecoaches, and on board vessels. His absorbing interest in hymn writing can be felt in his own words. Once after being thrown from a horse Charles recounted "my companions thought I had broken my neck, but my leg only was bruised, my hand sprained and my head stunned, which spoiled my making of hymns until the next day."

Charles married Sarah Gwynne (who was 19 years younger than Charles) in 1749 and his wife accompanied him on his journeys until they finally settled in Bristol in 1756. He then took on the task of overseeing the Methodist Societies in Bristol and London. Charles and Sarah had three children (Sarah, Charles, and Samuel) born between 1759 and 1766. In 1771, Charles moved his family to London where he remained until his death in 1788, the result of nervous exhaustion brought on by his high intensity lifestyle. He was still dictating his last hymn to Sarah even on his deathbed.

Both Charles and John understood something of the value of sacred song in impressing religious truths upon the hearts and minds of people. Charles learned a form of shorthand from John Byrom and usually scribbled his hymn poems rapidly. He seldom took time to polish his works, including "Hark! The Herald Angels Sing," which he wrote in 1739, one year after his religious conversion. George Whitefield and Martin Madan later revised some of Charles' original words to create the Christmas hymn, as we know it today. Charles did not even give his hymn an official title, but merely referred to it as a 'Hymn for Christmas Day.' An 18th century printer ignorantly inserted this Christmas hymn into the Church of England's 'Book of Common Prayer' after the Wesley's had left the Anglican Church to establish Methodism. Attempts were later made to remove the hymn from the 'Book of Common Prayer,' but because of its popularity, it was allowed to remain. It is said that Charles was inspired to write this hymn by the joyous chiming of bells in London as he walked to church. His text first appeared in "Hymns and Sacred Poems" in London in 1739. The hymn text as we know it today first appeared in the 'New Version Psalter' in 1782 during Charles' lifetime.

"Hark! The Herald Angels Sing" was sung to various tunes for more than a century until in 1855 William Cummings made his arrangement for the hymn 116 years after Charles had penned the original words.

RICHARD STORRS WILLIS

Composer of music for "It Came Upon the Midnight Clear" in 1850

Born on February 10, 1819 in Boston, Massachusetts
Died on May 7, 1900 in Detroit, Michigan

Richard Storrs Willis was one of nine children born to Nathaniel and Hannah (Parker) Willis. Nathaniel Willis was the founder of 'The Youth's Companion' journal, which he published and edited from 1827-57. Richard was also the younger brother of his more famous sibling, the poet, Nathaniel Parker Willis (1806-1867). As with other notable Christmas music creators, Richard's family was descended from some of the earliest European settlers in America. George Willis, described as a 'Puritan of considerable distinction,' arrived in New England in 1630 and settled in the newly established town of Cambridge, Massachusetts. Richard's father moved the family to Boston in 1812, and Richard was born there in 1819.

Richard was a fairly well known musician during the 19th century. His schooling took place first at Chauncey Hall, then at the Boston Latin School, and finally at Yale University, where he received a B.A. in 1841. At Yale, Richard served as president of the Beethoven Society, and wrote original musical compositions and arrangements for the first ever student orchestra at Yale. Part of Richard's musical training included six years of composition in Germany where he studied under S. von Wartensee in Frankfurt, and Xavier Schnyder and Moritz Hauptmann in Leipzig. During this same period of time Richard became an intimate friend of Felix Mendelssohn who had taken an interest in Richard's compositions. After Richard returned to the United States in 1848, due to continent wide revolutions in Europe, he served as a music critic for the 'New York Tribune' and 'The Albion,' and an editor of 'The Musical Times,' 'The Music World,' and the 'Once a Month' newspapers between 1852-64.

His own publications included 'Church Chorals and Choir Studies' in 1850. In this collection of hymns was included the tune 'Carol,' which would come to be used and find fame with the hymn "It Came Upon the Midnight Clear" by Edmund Hamilton Sears. The tune was originally used with another hymn text "See Israel's Gentle Shepherd Stand," with the tune name "Study No. 23," before being adapted to the famous Christmas hymn by Sears. Richard wrote a letter to his publisher in 1887 and said "Study No. 23 has undergone various changes. I expanded it first into a 'Christmas Carol' while a vestryman in the 'Church of the Transfiguration.'"

Other publications by Richard included 'Our Church Music' in 1856, 'Waif of Song' in 1876, and 'Pen and Lute' in 1883, however, it is his musical contribution of the tune "Carol" to "It Came Upon the Midnight Clear," composed while he was pursuing a journalistic career in New York City, for which he is primarily remembered today. He composed many lyrics and instrumental pieces, of which, "The Glen-Mary Waltzes," he stated, "were chiefly meritorious for their subsequent sale for 25 years, and the handsome returns they brought publisher and composer."

Richard married Anne Jeannette Cairns in 1851 and they had three children by the names of Annie, Blanche, and Jesse. Unfortunately, Anne died just one week after the birth of their third daughter, Jesse. Richard was remarried in 1861 to Alexandrine Macomb Sheldon, who survived Richard by ten years. If you would like to know more about the life of Richard Willis, he wrote an autobiographical sketch for the publishers, Bigelow and Main, which is now preserved in the Library of Congress. In this he tells of his student activity at Yale, and of arrangements as well as original compositions, which he made for the student orchestra. He further describes his six student years in Germany.

At the time of his death in Detroit, Michigan, at the age of 81, the life expectancy of a white male living in the United States was 48 years of age and the average annual income of an American was $637. The average price of a home was $4,000, and only one home in thirteen owned a telephone, but a lucky one in seven homeowners had a bathtub inside their house. Cars averaged $500 and a loaf of bread cost 3 cents per loaf. It was indeed a different world from today as America entered the 20th century and noted the passing of Richard Storrs Willis.

CATHERINE WINKWORTH

Translator of multiple German Christmas Hymns to English in 1855 and 1858

Born on September 13, 1827 in
Holborn, London, England
Died on July 1, 1878 near Geneva, Switzerland

Catherine Winkworth was born to Henry and Susanna (Dickenson) Winkworth in London. Her father was a silk mill owner, however, the family moved to Manchester, England when she was just two years old. Catherine lived a normal and healthy lifestyle during her first twenty years, but beginning in January of 1848, Catherine suffered through a tough two-year period of prolonged illness. Once fully recovered, she undertook active work among the poor in 1852 and was well respected by the poor in Manchester the remainder of her life. She lived in Manchester until 1862 when she moved with her father and sisters to Clifton, near Bristol, after her father's health broke and he had to give up his silk business. In Clifton, Catherine became active in promoting higher education for women and this interest led her to publish, in 1863, translations from German to English of biographies of the founders of sisterhoods for the poor and the sick.

Catherine's interest in German hymns was sparked by Chevelier Bunsen, a German ambassador to England, who presented her with a copy of a German devotional book filled with German hymns. In 1855 she published her famous "Lyra Germanica" collection of German hymns translated into English. She published a second volume of translated German hymns in 1858. In 1863, Catherine published "The Chorale Book for England" which contained some of her earliest translations with their proper chorale tunes in four-part harmony. She published "Christian Singers of Germany" in 1869, which contained the biographies of German hymn-writers.

Catherine is considered the foremost 19th century translator of German hymns to English. More than any other single person, she helped bring the German chorale tradition to the English-speaking world. Her translations are still the most widely used and are used extensively in many denominational hymnals, especially Lutheran ones.
Her successful translations are due to the fact that they were faithful to the text and spirit of the original songs and she used good English verse.

Catherine had traveled to Geneva, Switzerland on June 17, 1878. She was with a friend to help care for her friends' invalid nephew, but Catherine died suddenly from a heart attack on July 1, 1878. A tablet on the wall of Bristol Cathedral indicates that Catherine "opened a new source of light, consolation, and strength in many thousand homes."

Examples of her German Christmas hymn translations include Martin Luther's "From Heaven Above" and "Ah, Dearest Jesus, Holy Child" from 1855 and "All My Heart This Night Rejoices" and "All Praise To Thee, Eternal Lord" from 1858.

Catherine made the most of her fifty plus years and in doing so wrote her name in the music history books. She truly was an inspiring 'pioneer' for women in the field of music and we are the beneficiaries of her dedicated work. Thank you, Catherine Winkworth, for being a loving, caring, and talented lady.

JOHN FREEMAN YOUNG

English Translator of "Silent Night" in 1863

Born on October 30, 1820 in Pittston, Maine
Died on November 15, 1885 in New York, New York

John Freeman Young did 'one thing' to put his name permanently in the books of music history by translating the German "Stille Nacht! Heilige Nacht!" into the English Christmas hymn "Silent Night," he made a lasting gift to all English-speaking Christians. Unfortunately, not much is known of John's family or the first twenty years of his life, but from what we know of the remainder of his life, I think it's safe to say he was a good student and an industrious young man. John was born in Pittston, Maine, to John and Emma Young in the very year that Maine became a state and joined the United States of America. The U.S. population at the time was 9.6 million.

John began his higher education by enrolling for a scientific course at Wesleyan University in 1841, but left that institution during his freshman year. Soon after, he became a student in the Virginia Theological Seminary at Alexandria, from where he was graduated in 1845. He was then ordained into the ministry at the St. John's Protestant-Episcopal Church in Jacksonville, Florida. From there, he moved on to various posts in Texas, Mississippi and Louisiana before becoming an assistant rector at the Trinity Church in New York City from 1855-67. While in that position, John became a serious student of theology, church architecture and hymnology, and began collecting and translating great Christian hymns of various churches. He did take time out of his busy work schedule to court and marry Harriet B. Ogden in 1860 (she died in 1877), about the same time he made his famous translation of "Silent Night," which is the most widely used English translation in the United States. His translation first appeared in Clark Hollister's "Service and Tune Book" of 1863. This same English version of "Silent Night" first appeared in an American hymnal in 1871, but it was not until John's hymn collection titled "Great Hymns of the Church" was published in 1887 that his English translation of the song was officially credited to him.

John became the second Protestant-Episcopal Bishop of Florida in 1867, a position he held until his death. When elected to the post of Bishop, the diocese was only 29 years old and had been devastated by the effects of the Civil War. According to John, the first ten years of his episcopate were "mainly a struggle for life," but with the end of the depression of 1873 and the beginning of a wave of immigration into Florida, the diocese began to grow rapidly. John did much of the work of planting new missions himself. He traveled the state on horseback, in buggies and carts, by steamer and sailboat, and sometimes on foot to start missions wherever he found a few Episcopal families residing in close proximity. In Key West he organized the first Florida Episcopal Church exclusively for black people, and also a Spanish language parish for Cuban immigrants. John died from pneumonia at the age of 65 while on a trip to New York City, the very city where he created his famous translation of "Silent Night" twenty-six years earlier in 1859. His 2nd wife (m. 1879), Mary (Finley), survived him.

Thank you, John Freeman Young, for giving us the beautiful, peaceful English words to the most famous worldwide Christmas hymn "Silent Night."

They Overcame Personal Obstacles to Write Their Names in History Books

ADAM	his father discouraged his desire to become a musician—financial difficulties
ALEXANDER	poor eyesight—extreme shyness
CAPPEAU	lost his right hand in an accident at the age of eight
DWIGHT	emotional problems leading to panic attacks—premature death of his wife
GAUNTLETT	his father discouraged him from becoming a professional musician
GRUBER	his first wife died young
HANDEL	his father disapproved of music—blindness
HOLLAND	poverty—limited early educational opportunities
LONGFELLOW	premature death of his first wife and accidental death of second wife
LUTHER	poverty—branded a heretic by the church and an outlaw by the state
MASON	his parents discouraged his desire to become a musician
MENDELSSOHN	fragile health due to overwork
MOHR	poverty - poor health
MONTGOMERY	parents died when he was young, dismissed from school, imprisoned
NEALE	his father died when he was five—lifelong fragile health—semi-invalid
OAKELEY	poor eyesight—lame—involved in religious controversy
PIERPONT	wanderlust—poverty
REDNER	he joined the working world at age sixteen
ROSSETTI	prolonged illnesses from angina, tuberculosis, Grave's disease and cancer
SEARS	labors of farm life—prolonged illness—depression
SMART	poor lifelong eyesight—blindness
STAINER	blinded in one eye as a five year old boy
TATE	financial problems
WADE	he was exiled in France because of his political beliefs
WATTS	smallpox—prolonged illness—invalid
WESLEY	poverty
WINKWORTH	prolonged illness in her early twenties

More Great Christmas Books from Centerstream...

CHRISTMAS SOUTH OF THE BORDER
featuring the Red Hot Jalapeños
with special guest
The Cactus Brothers
Add heat to your holiday with these ten salsa-flavored arrangements of time-honored Christmas carols. With the accompanying CD, you can play your guitar along with The Cactus Brothers on: Jingle Bells • Deck the Halls • Silent Night • Joy to the World • What Child Is This? • and more. ¡Feliz Navidad!

00000319 Book/CD Pack $19.95

A CLASSICAL CHRISTMAS
by Ron Middlebrook
This book/CD pack features easy to advanced play-along arrangements of 23 top holiday tunes for classical/fingerstyle guitar. Includes: Birthday of a King • God Rest Ye, Merry Gentlemen • Good Christian Men, Rejoice • Jingle Bells • Joy to the World • O Holy Night • O Sanctissima • What Child Is This? (Greensleeves) • and more. The CD features a demo track for each song.

00000271 Book/CD Pack $15.95

CHRISTMAS UKULELE, HAWAIIAN STYLE
Play your favorite Christmas songs Hawaiian style with expert uke player Chika Nagata. This book/CD pack includes 12 songs, each played 3 times: the first and third time with the melody, the second time without the melody so you can play or sing along with the rhythm-only track. Songs include: Mele Kalikimaka (Merry Christmas to You) • We Wish You a Merry Christmas • Jingle Bells (with Hawaiian lyrics) • Angels We Have Heard on High • Away in a Manger • Deck the Halls • Hark! The Herald Angels Sing • Joy to the World • O Come, All Ye Faithful • Silent Night • Up on the Housetop • We Three Kings.

00000472 Book/CD Pack $19.95

JAZZ GUITAR CHRISTMAS
by George Ports
Features fun and challenging arrangements of 13 Christmas favorites. Each song is arranged in both easy and intermediate chord melody style. Songs include: All Through the Night • Angels from the Realm of Glory • Away in a Manger • The Boar's Head Carol • The Coventry Carol • Deck the Hall • Jolly Old St. Nicholas • and more.

00000240 .... $9.95

CHRISTMAS SOUTH OF THE BORDER
featuring The Cactus Brothers
with Special Guest
Señor Randall Ames
Add heat to your holiday with these Salsa-flavored piano arrangements of time-honored Christmas carols. Play along with the arrangements of Señor Randall Ames on Silent Night, Carol of the Bells, We Three Kings, Away in a Manger, O Come O Come Immanuel, and more. Feliz Navidad!

00000343 Book/CD Pack $19.95
00000345 Book/CD Pack $19.95

DOBRO CHRISTMAS
arranged by Stephen F. Toth
Well, it's Christmas time again, and you, your family and friends want to hear some of those favorite Christmas songs on your glistening (like the "trees") Dobro with its bell-like (as in "jingle") tone. This book contains, in tablature format, 2 versions of 20 classic Christmas songs plus a bonus "Auld Lang Syne" for your playing and listening pleasure. The arrangements were created to make them easy to learn, play, remember, or sight read. So get playing and get merry!

00000218 .... $9.95

CHRISTMAS MUSIC COMPANION FACT BOOK
by Dale V. Nobbman
For 50 beloved traditional tunes, readers will learn the story of how the song came to be, the author and the historical setting, then be able to play a great arrangement of the song! Songs examined include: Away in a Manger • Deck the Halls • Jingle Bells • Joy to the World • O Christmas Tree • O Holy Night • Silver Bells • We Wish You a Merry Christmas • What Child Is This? • and more!

00000272 112 pages $12.95

THE ULTIMATE CHRISTMAS MUSIC COMPANION FACT BOOK
by Dale Nobbman
This book provides comprehensive biographical sketches of the men and women who wrote, composed, and translated the most famous traditional Christmas songs of all time. Their true-life stories and achievements are fascinating and inspirational for anyone wanting to know more about the people behind the music. 144 pages.

00001178 .... $24.95

P.O. Box 17878 - Anaheim Hills, CA 92817

(714) 779-9390   www.centerstream-usa.com

    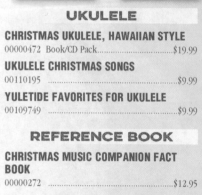